# THE
# UNDERGROUND
# RAILROAD

NEW EDITION

# THE UNDERGROUND RAILROAD

## NEXT STOP, TORONTO!

**Adrienne Shadd, Afua Cooper, and Karolyn Smardz Frost**

DUNDURN
PRESS

Publisher: Scott Fraser | Acquiring editor: Kathryn Lane | Editor: Laurie Miller
Cover designer: Karen Alexiou | Interior designer: Laura Boyle
Cover images: (top left) View of King Street, ca. 1844, showing Thornton Blackburn's yellow and red cab. John Gillespie, artist. Courtesy of Royal Ontario Museum.
(top right) From Samuel Ringgold Ward, *Autobiography of a Fugitive Negro: His Anti-Slavery Labors in the United States, Canada, and England* (London, U.K.: John Snow, 1855), frontispiece.
(bottom left) Courtesy of Library of Congress, LOT 15020.
(middle right) From William Still, *The Underground Rail Road* (Philadelphia: Porter & Coates, 1872), opp. 561.
(bottom right) Toronto Public Library (TRL), John Ross Robertson Collection, T32137.

Printer: Marquis Book Printing Inc.

**Library and Archives Canada Cataloguing in Publication**

Title: The underground railroad : next stop, Toronto! / Adrienne Shadd, Afua Cooper, and Karolyn Smardz Frost.
Names: Shadd, Adrienne L. (Adrienne Lynn), 1954- author. | Cooper, Afua, author. | Smardz Frost, Karolyn, author.
Description: New edition. | Includes bibliographical references and index.
Identifiers: Canadiana (print) 20210335432 | Canadiana (ebook) 20210335440 | ISBN 9781459748965 (softcover) | ISBN 9781459748972 (PDF) | ISBN 9781459748989 (EPUB)
Subjects: LCSH: Underground Railroad—Ontario—Toronto. | LCSH: Toronto (Ont.)—History—19th century. | CSH: Black Canadians—Ontario—Toronto—History—19th century.
Classification: LCC FC3097.9.B6 S43 2022 | DDC j971.3/54100496—dc23

We acknowledge the support of the Canada Council for the Arts and the Ontario Arts Council for our publishing program. We also acknowledge the financial support of the Government of Ontario, through the Ontario Book Publishing Tax Credit and Ontario Creates, and the Government of Canada.

Care has been taken to trace the ownership of copyright material used in this book. The author and the publisher welcome any information enabling them to rectify any references or credits in subsequent editions.

The publisher is not responsible for websites or their content unless they are owned by the publisher.

Printed and bound in Canada.

Dundurn Press
1382 Queen Street East
Toronto, Ontario, Canada M4L 1C9
dundurn.com, @dundurnpress 𝕏 f ⊚

For the freedom seekers and their descendants.

## CAUTION!!!

From information received from reliable sources, we learn that parties are at present in Toronto, endeavouring to induce colored persons to go to the States in their employ as servants. From the character of the propositions, there is reason to believe that "foul play" is intended. Possibly, that Constable Pope's designs on the fugitives and others are being carried out.

Individuals have proposed to women to go to Detroit to live in their service, and another party under circumstances of great suspicion, to a boy to go as far South as Philadelphia. We say to our people, listen to no flattering proposals of the sort. You are in Canada, and let no misplaced confidence in this or the other smooth-tongued Yankee, or British subject either, who may be mercenary enough to ensnare you into bondage by collusion with kidnappers in the States, deprive you of your liberty ...

— An excerpt from the *Provincial Freeman*, April 21, 1851.

# CONTENTS

# A WORD FROM THE ONTARIO BLACK HISTORY SOCIETY

THE OFFICE OF THE Ontario Black History Society at 10 Adelaide Street East overlooks the Adelaide Courtyard, which is the site where James Mink, a Black man whose parents had been enslaved in Upper Canada (present-day Ontario), operated two of several successful businesses: the Mansion House Hotel and a livery stable. From his vantage point as a long-time Toronto resident, he witnessed the influx of freedom seekers who settled into the emerging city centre and was an active member of Toronto's growing Black community. Mink was involved in the annual celebration in Toronto of Emancipation Day, leading an Emancipation Day parade in the 1850s through the principal streets of the city in a carriage drawn by eight well-groomed horses.

Mink's story is illustrative of the ways that Black history blankets the city's landscape, though obscured by the vast urbanization of Canada's largest city and its erasure of the Black Canadian presence. There is an over-220-year presence of Black people in what is now the city of Toronto; this extends outward from the city core to the modern-day city limits. The Underground Railroad era saw the first large wave of African-descended refugees into Toronto in pursuit of their freedom. Hundreds of freedom seekers chose the city as their permanent or temporary home, contributing to the development and growth of Toronto and to the fabric of a diverse, thriving Black community.

The Ontario Black History Society is honoured to continue to play a pivotal role in the preservation and dissemination of this extensive history, contributing to the foundational scholarship of such early researchers of Black history in Toronto as our co-founder Dr. Daniel G. Hill and past president Rosemary Sadlier. One of the highlights of our work was collaborating with Parks Canada to develop "The Underground Railroad: Next Stop Freedom!," an exhibit that launched in 2002 and is now permanently installed in the Oakville Museum at the Erchless Estate. This project spurred the publication of the first edition of *The Underground Railroad: Next Stop, Toronto!* to record and share the rich heritage of people of African descent in Toronto and to make their history more accessible. This publication brought to light an array of stories of nineteenth-century Black Toronto and situated them in the largest freedom movement in North America.

Over the past twenty years, many more stories of Black Canadian history in Toronto have been unearthed, some of them literally. There were the 2015 archaeological excavations for the new Toronto courthouse on Armoury Street that included the site of the British Methodist Episcopal Church on Chestnut Street and homes of several freedom seekers and Underground Railroad operatives. More has been learned about early Black residents such as freedom seeker Joshua Glover, who settled in Etobicoke, and other Black men and women who raised families, established community institutions, and participated in all facets of society.

The enduring popularity of *The Underground Railroad: Next Stop, Toronto!* and its reprint speaks to the impact, reach, and relevance of Black Canadian history and the skillful scholarship of Karolyn Smardz Frost, Afua Cooper, and Adrienne Shadd. The significance of this text is even more timely this year after the social uprisings during the spring and summer of 2020 against widespread anti-Black racism and its legacies that have impacted Black life in Toronto, in Ontario, in

Canada, and beyond. These historical narratives contextualize current realities, honour Black Canadian contributions and accomplishments, and help us to envision and implement transformational change for the betterment of Black futures.

This influential book maps a diverse Black presence on the urban terrain. It underscores the urgent need for mandated learning expectations in the Ontario curriculum of the four-hundred-year presence of Black people in Canada. The impact of *Next Stop, Toronto!* also highlights the need for a museum and cultural centre in Toronto that centres and interprets Black Canadian history in a nuanced way. These glaring gaps have been made more visible in the current social and political climate. The OBHS recognizes the importance of knowledge-building in the efforts to advance social justice and we applaud the substantial contribution that *The Underground Railroad: Next Stop, Toronto!* makes in educating the wider public. It has become essential reading on Black history in Canada, and we are ever grateful to Smardz Frost, Cooper, and Shadd for their endeavour.

Natasha Henry
President, Ontario Black History Society

# INTRODUCTION

The colored people in Toronto are, on the whole, remarkably in-
dustrious. Their condition is such as to gratify the philanthropist,
and afford encouragement to the friends of emancipation everywhere. A portion of them sustain a lyceum or debating club (which
is attended by both sexes) where debates are held, and original
essays read. A large majority of the adult colored people are refugees from the South …[1]

— BENJAMIN DREW, 1856

SLAVERY EXISTED IN NORTH AMERICA almost from the time of the first
European settlement on this continent. At first, it was Indigenous people who
were bound to unwilling and unpaid labour, but soon European colonizers sought
new resources. Starting with Africans enslaved by the Spanish in the 1520s and
those brought for the settlement of St. Augustine, Florida, in 1565, millions of
people were stolen from their homes in Africa to be sold in the markets of the

Americas. In 1619, "twenty and odd" Africans were purchased from a British privateer ship and enslaved at Virginia's Jamestown Colony. This began British North America's 250-year-long history of human bondage.

The first African believed to have set foot on Canadian soil was a free man named Mathieu Da Costa. Speaking several languages, he served as an interpreter for Samuel de Champlain on his 1604 voyage. Starting in 1629 with a little boy from Madagascar who took the name Olivier Le Jeune at Quebec City, first French and then British Canada enslaved Africans. Torn from home and family and often first forced to work in the West Indies or the Thirteen Colonies (colonial America), they were imported to serve the colonists of New France, in the fisheries and farms of the Maritime provinces, and in the households of Upper Canada (what is now Ontario).

After the American Revolution, most northern U.S. states began to see the contradiction between depending upon this unpaid labour system and the freedom promised in the new American Constitution. By 1800, some northern states and Upper Canada had moved toward gradually ending slavery. However, the institution continued to enrich slaveholders in the largely agricultural American south, especially after the 1793 invention of the cotton gin. This "gin," or engine, combed the tiny, sticky seeds out of cotton fibres far more quickly than people could do it by hand, making cotton plantation agriculture immensely profitable.

Africans resisted enslavement from the very moment they were captured and forced onto ships to be transported to the Americas. Many other people thought slavery was wrong, too. Some religious groups, such as the Society of Friends (known as the Quakers), preached against enslaving other people. Beginning in the mid-1700s in England, the United States, and Canada, Black and white individuals called "abolitionists" stood forth to oppose slavery. They established anti-slavery organizations, published pamphlets and books, gave public lectures, and pressured politicians to try to have slavery made illegal. But this forced labour system was very profitable, and many people in the northern states would not accept even free African Americans as equal citizens. Laws were passed to prevent

Black Americans from gaining an education, participating in the political process, or even deciding where they could live and work. Over time, Southerners who supported slavery came to pretend that African Americans could not take care of themselves if they were not enslaved. So slavery itself came to be seen by some white people as beneficial. But this was a lie to serve the financial interests of wealthy slaveholders.

Because of the gradual abolition law that was passed in Upper Canada in 1793 and later decisions made by the courts that limited slavery in Quebec, Nova Scotia, and New Brunswick, the provinces of Canada — especially Upper Canada — became the primary destination of African Americans trying to escape from slavery. Called by those claiming their service "fugitive slaves," today we know these brave individuals as "freedom seekers," people who risked everything to liberate themselves.

Britain ended slavery throughout most of her Empire by the Slavery Abolition Act passed in 1833. Reaching Canada, many formerly enslaved people, especially those who had previously lived on farms and plantations in the United States, wanted to purchase their own farmland and live independently. Rural colonies of freedom seekers such as the Elgin Settlement at Buxton, the Dawn Settlement at Dresden, and the Refuge Home Society near Windsor were testimony to the deep desire of Black newcomers arriving in Canada West to own and operate their own farms and govern their own communities.

However, other people who had lived in the urban centres of the southern and northern United States had skills and abilities best suited to city life. Hairdressers, barbers, seamstresses, cooks, carpenters, bricklayers, masons, and other skilled tradespeople found jobs, opened businesses, and established a vibrant community right in the heart of what is now Canada's largest city, Toronto. And so the title for this book is *The Underground Railroad: Next Stop, Toronto!*

Most people do not think of Toronto as a major "terminus" (or final destination) of the Underground Railroad. Yet before Union victory in the Civil War ended slavery in the United States in 1865, at least fifteen hundred Black people

Underground Railroad
routes to Toronto.

had settled in the downtown core and on the outskirts of the growing urban centre. There they developed a rich and complex "world-within-a-world," creating active social, intellectual, political, charitable, and religious institutions and organizations.

British North America was reorganized after British losses in the American Revolutionary War. Upper Canada was formed out of much of what today is Ontario. The new province gained both a new Lieutenant Governor, John Graves Simcoe, and in 1793 the capital he named the "Town of York." When refugees from American bondage first arrived in the Town of York they found a very different city from the one that we know today. Up to the 1850s, most houses and stores were built of wood, although there were wealthy people's homes, and large and impressive public buildings built of fine red brick. Originally the main business district spread out east from Yonge, between King Street and Lake Ontario.

King Street east of Yonge was the fashionable shopping area. From today's Dufferin Street on the west to the Don River on the east, the whole area above Queen as far north as Bloor Street was divided up into huge private estates known as "Park Lots." There were few residential streets north of Queen, although this would begin to change from the 1830s onward, when the families who owned Park Lots began dividing them up for sale. The part of town from Dundas Street north to Bloor, which was then the city limits, was farmland and bush.

In 1834, the old Town of York was incorporated into Upper Canada's first real city. It regained its original First Nations name of "Toronto" and had a population of about nine thousand. Upper Canada (Ontario) and Lower Canada (Quebec) were organized into the new Province of Canada. Toronto became part of Canada West after the Act of Union in 1840.

In the following year, Peter Gallego, an African Canadian student at King's College who had been asked to take a census of Black Torontonians, presented his findings. He counted 535 people of African descent in the city, but there were still more living in the "Liberties," as the areas to the west, north, and east of the urban core were known.

Early African Canadian Toronto included the descendants of those formerly enslaved by British and United Empire Loyalist settlers, along with Black Loyalists and some people from the West Indies. But by far the largest proportion of the Black population by the 1850s was made up of immigrants from the United States. The majority were freedom seekers from the American South who sought new homes and new lives in freedom. These were joined by educated and propertied free Black families from both the North and the South, especially after 1850 when their continued liberty in their American homes was threatened by the passage of the U.S. Congress's harsh new Fugitive Slave Law.[2]

After the U.S. Civil War (1861–65), Canada was confederated (joined) into a new nation, and the old Upper Canada/Canada West region became "Ontario." Some Blacks returned to the U.S. over time, often in search of family and friends they had left behind, but others remained in Toronto. In the early twentieth century, a new wave of Black immigrants came from the American South to work on the Canadian Pacific and Canadian National Railways. Immigrants from the Caribbean also began to trickle into Toronto and other Canadian cities in larger numbers. However, in 1911 the Canadian government passed an act to prevent people it deemed "unfit" from coming into Canada. A profoundly racist piece of legislation, this included people of African descent. It wasn't until this law was changed in the 1960s that Blacks, mostly from Jamaica and other Caribbean countries, began to settle here by the thousands. In the twenty-first century, Black newcomers to Canada come from 125 different countries, most of them in Africa. Today Toronto has the largest population of people of African ancestry in all of Canada.[3]

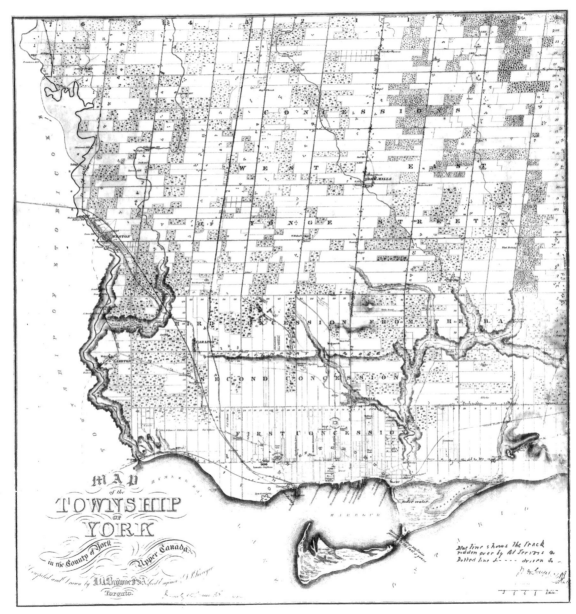

Map of Toronto and York Township East and West, 1852.

Deborah Brown was
one of the many who
came to Canada via the
Underground Railroad.

# one

# DEBORAH BROWN: FREEDOM SEEKER

ON DECEMBER 8, 1908, the *Evening Telegram* published the story of an elderly woman named Deborah Brown who lived in a part of Toronto known as Seaton Village. Mrs. Brown had died in 1898 and is reported to have been 111 years old at the time of her death. She was considered to be the oldest resident in Seaton Village, and her house was said to be the oldest building in the village. Deborah Brown had once been enslaved in Maryland, on the east coast of the United States. She had escaped to Canada in the mid-1800s with her husband, Perry, when they learned he was about to be sold. The couple moved to the Township of York, the part of Toronto north of Bloor Street, which was the northern edge of the City of Toronto at the time. She lived in the same one-storey wooden cottage on Markham Street, near the corner of Bathurst and Bloor Streets, for over fifty years.

Deborah Brown's cottage at 691 Markham Street, shown here, was the oldest house in Seaton Village.

Nowadays it is hard for us to imagine that when Deborah and Perry Brown first moved to the area, it was rural farmland. By the 1870s their neighbourhood, by then known as "Seaton Village," was bounded by Bedford Road on the east, Christie Street on the west, and Davenport Road to the north, with Bloor Street as its southern perimeter. In 1888, Seaton Village and the Town of Yorkville, which had developed just to the east around Yonge and Bloor Streets, were annexed to the growing city of Toronto. In a span of fifty years, the region where the Browns lived had gone from being on the rural fringes to being in the centre of the city.

Deborah Brown worked as a washerwoman, and her husband was a labourer. The Browns were a working-class family, judging from their occupations and their standard of living. Deborah could not read or write, and her husband, Perry, was also probably illiterate. In most U.S. states it was illegal to teach an enslaved person to read and write, so they had likely been prevented from gaining an education before coming to Canada. They purchased the house and the quarter-acre lot on which they lived for $50 in 1870. Their house was a modest wooden cottage with a garden, and they owned two pigs. Deborah and Perry were part of a larger Black community that was comprised of a working class, a middle class of skilled craftsmen and shop owners, and a tiny upper class of wealthy families whose businesses had been very successful. These wealthier Black Torontonians often owned a great deal of property, including houses that they rented out.

Deborah's work as a washerwoman was one of the jobs that women did to earn money, but it was hard, backbreaking work. Prior to the invention of electric washers and dryers, washing clothes involved hauling and heating a large bucket of water and mixing in a lye-based soap. Clothes had to be washed by hand, then rinsed, dried, and ironed. Many women were able to earn a living by taking in other people's laundry. However, Mrs. Brown lived during the Victorian era of the 1800s. At that time a woman's primary responsibility was her own household, and it was frowned upon if a woman engaged in waged work. Nevertheless, most Black women had always worked. Their income was needed to help support the family.

In the late 1870s, Mrs. Brown was listed in the city directory as a nurse. This "directory" was a book published each year that recorded the name, address, and occupation of the head of each Toronto household. It is not likely that she studied nursing formally, as formal training in nursing did not begin in Toronto until the 1880s. Deborah may have gained a great deal of knowledge over the years in curing various sicknesses through the use of herbs, roots, and the like, and used her knowledge to nurse friends and acquaintances back to health. However, many women who reported their occupations as nurses in the nineteenth century were untrained. They worked in what today is known as personal support work, looking after the sick and elderly, cooking, and keeping the house tidy. This occupation was pursued especially by women who were widowed after the death of their husbands. It was another way to survive, and Deborah, too, found this avenue for earning a living.

Deborah and Perry were of the Wesleyan Methodist faith. They probably attended the Black churches in downtown Toronto from time to time — certainly on special occasions like Christmas, Easter, and Emancipation Day, the day set aside in early August to celebrate the British act of parliament of 1833 that freed enslaved people in most of the British Empire. However, Deborah also attended the Methodist church in Seaton Village. The 1908 *Evening Telegram* article notes that even in extreme old age Mrs. Brown continued to be a member of the Sunday School. She delighted in getting up on the platform with the children at Sunday School anniversary celebrations. Most Black people at that time belonged to either the Methodist or the Baptist faith, although there were Anglicans, Catholics, Presbyterians, and Congregationalists in the community, too.

Deborah Brown had at least one child that we know of. Her name was Sarah Brooks, but she does not seem to have come with her parents when they escaped to Canada. Sadly, her parents may have been forced by circumstances to leave her behind in slavery. There was, however, an eight-year-old child named William H. Brown, born in the United States, who lived with Deborah and Perry in 1861. Because of Deborah's age then, fifty-six, it is not certain whether William was her child or a grandchild. He may even have been a nephew or great-nephew. When the census was taken in 1861 listing nearly all the people in every household in Canada, William H. was reported to be absent from the Brown home and living in "Toronto City" attending school. Unfortunately, after 1861, William was not listed in the same household as Deborah Brown again, and we are not sure what happened to him.

More is known about daughter Sarah Brooks. She had been born in the United States and she in turn had a daughter named Cornelia, who was also American-born.

After the American Civil War was over and once-enslaved African Americans were free, these two women were living on Centre Street in St. John's Ward, just west of today's City Hall. According to the 1881 census, Sarah was fifty-six and Cornelia (her name was mistakenly recorded by the census-taker as "Amelia") was twenty-three years of age. Both were widows. Like Deborah, her daughter and granddaughter also worked as laundresses.

On January 1, 1863, Abraham Lincoln, president of the United States, issued the Emancipation Proclamation that freed all enslaved African Americans in the states that had rebelled against the Union. After the Civil War, with the passage of the Thirteenth Amendment to the American Constitution, all the enslaved people of the American South gained their freedom. Some people who had found refuge in what is now Ontario went back to the United States in search of the families and homes they had left behind.

However, the story of Deborah and Perry Brown and of their daughter Sarah Brooks shows that, rather than making a "return trip" south after the Civil War, some African Canadians brought their family members north to live with them in Canada.

On May 8, 2014, in recognition of Deborah Brown's long history and contribution to Toronto, city council named the laneway just east of Markham Street between Barton Avenue and London Street the Deborah Brown Laneway.

*Part of York, Upper Canada, 1804.* Elizabeth Frances Hale (1774–1832), artist.

# two

# BLACKS IN EARLY TORONTO

BLACK MEN, WOMEN, AND CHILDREN helped lay the foundations for the Town of York, as Toronto was briefly called. Situated in a sheltered harbour on the banks of Lake Ontario, it had been home to Indigenous Peoples for millennia. They called it "Toronto." By the 1740s, it was the site of the French Fort Rouillé and a centre for fur traders. In 1793, the new Lieutenant Governor of Upper Canada (later Ontario) John Graves Simcoe, established it as a military and shipbuilding base. In the wake of British losses in the American Revolution, the defence of British Canada was of the highest priority. Simcoe renamed the site the "Town of York," and by 1799 there were about twenty-five Blacks living in the town out of a population of about two hundred. In this very early period, Black men chopped down trees, helped to clear the forest, constructed buildings, built roads, and served in the army, while many women cared for the homes and children of European settlers.

Blacks in York came from diverse backgrounds and origins. There were Black Loyalists who had fought on the British side in the Revolutionary War and there

## THE LONG FAMILY

One free family was that of Peter and Sarah Long. Black Loyalist pioneer Peter Long was a free man originally from Massachusetts. A mast-maker and ship's carpenter, he fought as a gunner for the British forces during the Revolutionary War on a ship named *Nova Scotia*. After the war ended, Long settled first in New Brunswick and then in Darlington Township, Upper Canada. He and Sarah moved their family of ten to what is now Toronto in 1793. They made their first home in the old Town of York, receiving both a town lot and a two-hundred-acre land grant east of the Don River. Peter served in the War of 1812 doing construction work at Kingston, and his son James was in the navy. On July 18, 1818, James petitioned for both his now-deceased father and himself to be included in the United Empire Loyalist lists but was refused, an experience all too common amongst Black Loyalists who had bravely fought for the Crown during the American Revolution. Peter Long passed away in 1816, but his widow, Sarah, lived to see the old Town of York grow into the bustling city of Toronto. She died in 1856 and is buried in St. James Cemetery.

were both free and enslaved African Canadians within this population. There were also African Americans who had escaped to Canada seeking freedom. Some free African Americans also made York their home during this early period. There was a small number of Caribbean Blacks, as well.

Free Blacks were among the early road-builders of York and the rest of the province. In 1799, several Black men won the contract to build a road from Davenport Road to Castle Frank Road, just west of the Don River.[1] This thoroughfare was instrumental in linking the east and west ends of the town.

It should be noted that several important persons, such as Peter Russell, who temporarily administered Upper Canada following the departure of Simcoe, were slaveholders. Hannah and William Jarvis, who was the first provincial secretary of Upper Canada, also claimed the service of six enslaved people. Slavery

*Toronto from the Don River, 1855.* Mary Hastings Meyer, artist.

was not officially abolished in York and Upper Canada until after the British government's 1833 Emancipation Act took effect on August 1, 1834. It freed all those enslaved by British subjects in much of the Empire, most notably in the West Indies and Canada.

But life in York was changing — and so, too, for Black people. The War of 1812 led to an increase in the overall population of both Upper Canada and its capital, the Town of York. The war was fought between Britain and the United States, in part, over the ownership of Canada. York (Toronto) was twice invaded by the Americans. Many Black men from York and the rest of the province fought in the British army and militias in defence of Upper Canada, including an all-Black unit known as the Coloured Corps. After this war, more and more African

**MOSES HOLMES,**

FASHIONABLE HAIR CUTTER AND EASY SHAVER.

*King Street.*

RESPECTFULLY informs the Gentlemen of York, that he has commenced business as a Hair Dresser in that central shop west of the market square lately occupied by Mr. Mills the Hatter, where he solicits a share of public patronage, which he will endeavour to merit by the utmost attention to his customers.

M. H. invites the attention of the public to the annexed attestation of character which he received from Judge Parker and other gentlemen of high standing in Virginia. *Sept.* 27. 1831.                                    842

Moses Holmes the bearer hereof a free man of color who has resided some time in this place, as a slave, and within the last twelve months as a free man, is personally well known to us, and each of us; he sustains a fair character; we believe him strictly honest, and his deportment and conduct has been unexceptionable. We view him as an exception to persons in his situation in life; and as he is about to leave this place, we have freely and voluntarily offered him this testimonial of our regard and of the estimation in which we hold him. To whatever country he may go, we wish him success:        *Suffolk, 7th Sept.* 1824.

| | | |
|---|---|---|
| Joseph Prentis, | James Harrell, | John B. Parker, |
| Wm. Shepherd, | Willis Cowper, | N. D. Wright, |
| Rich'd Godwin, | Arthur Smith, | Henry Riddick, |
| Wm. D. Taylor, | John T. Kilby, | David Lawrence, |
| Eliott Whitehead, | Rich'd D. Webb, | John White, |
| Edgar Whitehead, | John B. Benton, | Augustus Morgan, |
| John C. Jenkins, | Wm. D. McClenny, | John C. Cohoon, |
| Arch'd D. Davis, | Thos. G. Benton, | John Murdough, |

I add my hearty assent to the above,

RICHARD E. PARKER,

*Judge of General 2nd Judicial Circuit Virginia.*

Advertisement for Moses Holmes's hairdressing establishment, *Colonial Advocate*, September 29, 1831.

Americans began to filter into Upper Canada. Returning American soldiers spread the word that that they had fought African Canadian soldiers on the borders of Upper Canada, and that Black people in British North America were free.

By 1828, the Black population in the city had grown in size and Blacks were now establishing themselves in several professions. One African Torontonian for whom there is some information is John Y. Butler, a barber, who opened a salon in 1825. It is reported that Butler became very successful at his job, so much so that, by 1827, he was employing white men and women as house servants and babysitters. William Lyon Mackenzie, reformer, politician, and newspaper publisher, mentioned this fact in his paper, the *Colonial Advocate*, on October 4, 1827.

A newspaper ad promotes another Black Toronto barber by the name of Moses Holmes. He originally came from Virginia and was a free man. This ad appeared in the *Colonial Advocate* in 1831.

The couple who would establish the first cab company in Toronto, Thornton and Lucie Blackburn, arrived in 1834. That year "York" was incorporated as a city and the name changed to "Toronto," derived from the Mohawk term *tkaronto*, "place where trees grow down to the water."[2]

By this date, the population was around nine thousand, with at least four hundred Blacks. The foundations were being laid for the building of significant community institutions such as businesses, churches, social reform societies, schools, and political organizations. By the middle of the century, many African Americans had found lives and new homes in the city.

Toronto Harbour, 1838, looking north from Maitland's Wharf at the foot of Church Street, showing the Ontario House Hotel and Wellington Street East in the background. William H. Bartlett, artist.

## THE POMPADOUR FAMILY

In contrast to the Long family, the wife and the children of Pompadour, a free Black, were en-slaved by Peter Russell and his sister Elizabeth. Russell became the provincial administrator after Simcoe's departure from Canada in 1796. The Pompadour family consisted of Peggy, the mother, three children — Jupiter, Milly, and Amy — and the father, known as Mr. Pompadour. He was employed by the Russell family for wages. Peggy and her children worked in the Russell household near Front and Princess Streets. However, they sometimes also undertook agricultural tasks on the family farm located north of Queen and Peter Streets.

Peggy hated slavery and tales of her resistance are nothing short of inspiring. Several times she tried to run away from the Russells. On one such occasion, Peter Russell responded by having Peggy jailed. In 1803, Russell wrote to Matthew Elliott, a white Loyalist slaveholder living at Amherstburg, near Windsor. Elliott had arranged to buy Peggy from Russell but seemed to be reneging on his promise. In the letter, Russell stated that he had paid £10 to have Peggy released from jail, but she had disappeared. He also said that his sister Elizabeth would not permit Peggy back in the Russell home. Russell was therefore anxious that the sale of Peggy, whom he described as "very troublesome," be completed with Elliott.

The sale did not go through, however, and Peggy remained with the Russells. Though Peggy was an adult woman, Peter Russell always called her just "Peggy," and did not use her last name. She was enslaved; her status was low. In 1806, Peter Russell tried again, placing an advertisement in the *Upper Canada Gazette* newspaper offering both Peggy and her son, Jupiter, for sale.

The advertisement provides an insight into the nature of work done by enslaved people in York. It indicates that Peggy cooked and washed for the Russells and also undertook tasks like soap- and candle-making, which were essential skills in Upper Canada's early years. Most likely her daughters, Milly and Amy, performed the same kinds of household duties. Her son, Jupiter, worked as a farm labourer, but also spent time in domestic service. Their daily responsibilities demonstrate that not only did their unwaged labour contribute to making the lives of one of York's wealthy white families more comfortable, but the Pompadours also helped in the building of the new society.

Peter Russell died in 1808 and passed on all his property, including the enslaved, to his sister Elizabeth. She gave Amy as a "gift" to her goddaughter Elizabeth Denison, who lived far from the Pompadour family in what today is Weston. Reverend Henry Scadding, in his history of early Toronto entitled *Toronto of Old*, notes that Amy Pompadour was one of several Blacks that people used to see around town when it was still called York. Scadding described her as a "tall, comely, Negress ... of servile descent" who, in the days when slavery was just dying out in Upper Canada, was quite a curiosity because of her still-enslaved status.

What became of one of the last enslaved families of Toronto? The *York Gazette* announced the death of Pompadour in its October 3, 1807, edition. It is believed that Peggy Pompadour died between 1827 and 1829: she had been receiving rations from the Society for the Relief of the Sick and Destitute, but her name stopped appearing on the list after August 1827 to March 1829. It is not known what happened to Jupiter or Milly, but Amy Pompadour had a son, Duke Denison, who was born in 1811 while Amy was still enslaved. He married in Toronto in 1835, lived on the outskirts of St. Patrick's Ward, and died in 1860 in Lewiston, New York. Amy Pompadour died an inmate of the Toronto House of Industry in 1865, at about eighty-five years of age.

> ## TO BE SOLD,
> A BLACK WOMAN, named PEGGY, aged about forty years ; and a Black boy her son, named JUPITER, aged about fifteen years, both of them the property of the Subfcriber.
>
> The Woman is a tolerable Cook and wafher woman and perfectly underftands making Soap and Candles.
>
> The Boy is tall and ftrong of his age, and has been employed in Country bufinefs, but brought up principally as a Houfe Servant—They are each of them Servants for life. The Price for the Woman is one hundred and fifty Dollars—for the Boy two hundred Dollars, payable in three years with Intereft from the day of Sale and to be properly fecured by Bond &c.— But one fourth lefs will be taken in ready Money.
>
> PETER RUSSELL.
>
> York, Feb. 10th 1806.

Peter Russell advertised Peggy and her son, Jupiter Pompadour, for sale on February 22, 1806.

A group of fifteen freedom seekers arriving by schooner at League Island just across from the city of Philadelphia, as depicted in William Still's *The Underground Rail Road*.

## three

# UNDERGROUND RAILROAD TO TORONTO

IN MARCH 1793, an enslaved woman named Chloe Cooley was bound and transported from the Niagara Region to the United States by her owner, Adam Vrooman. Although Cooley had screamed and resisted violently, there was nothing that the Executive Council of Upper Canada could do because she was legally enslaved. Her owner was perfectly within his rights to sell her to the United States (or anywhere else, for that matter). She was his property and could be bought and sold like any of his other personal belongings.

Lieutenant Governor John Graves Simcoe had just arrived in the province and was known to have abolitionist sympathies. He wanted to abolish slavery in the colony but was blocked from doing so due to the opposition among the slaveholding members of his executive council. However, Simcoe was able to pass a bill in July of that same year banning the importation of enslaved people into Upper Canada. Although the new act of the Upper Canadian parliament did not free anyone, it allowed for the eventual emancipation of their children. The *Act*

### CHAP. VII.

An Act to prevent the further introduction of SLAVES, and to limit the Term of Contracts for SERVITUDE within this Province.

[9th July, 1793.]

WHEREAS it is unjust that a people who enjoy Freedom by Law should encourage the introduction of Slaves, and whereas it is highly expedient to abolish Slavery in this Province, so far as the same may gradually be done without violating private property; Be it enacted by the King's Most Excellent Majesty, by and with the advice and consent of the Legislative Council and Assembly of the Province of Upper-Canada, constituted and assembled by virtue of and under the authority of an Act passed in the Parliament of Great-Britain, intituled, "An Act to repeal certain parts of an Act passed in the fourteenth year of His Majesty's Reign, intituled, ' An Act for making more effectual provision for the Government of the Province of Quebec, in North America, and to make further provision for the Government of the said Province," and by the authority of the same, ' That from and after the passing of this Act, so much of a certain Act of the Parliament of Great Britain, passed in the thirtieth year of His present Majesty, intituled "An Act for encouraging new Settlers in His Majesty's Colonies and Plantations in America." as may enable the Governor or Lieutenant Governor of this Province, heretofore parcel of His Majesty's Province of Quebec, to grant a licence for importing into the same any Negro or Negroes, shall be, and the same is hereby repealed; and that from and after the passing of this Act, it shall not be lawful for the Governor, Lieutenant Governor or Person administering the Government of this Province, to grant a licence for the importation of any Negro or other person to be subjected to the condition of a Slave, or to a bounden involuntary service for life, into any part of this Province; nor shall any Negro, or other person who shall come or be brought into this Province after the passing of this Act, be subject to the condition of a Slave, or to such service as aforesaid, within this Province, nor shall any voluntary contract of service or indentures that may be entered into by any parties within this Province, after the passing of this Act, be binding on them or either of them, for a longer time than a term of nine years, from the day of the date of such contract.

Excerpt from the parliamentary act to limit slavery as initiated in 1793 by Lieutenant Governor John Graves Simcoe. Statutes of Upper Canada Cap. 7, 33 George III, 1793.

*to Prevent the Further Introduction of Slaves and to Limit the Term of Contracts for Servitude Within This Province* ruled that those children would be free upon reaching the age of twenty-five years, and their own children were to be considered free-born.

Not one Upper Canadian slave was freed by Simcoe's *Act*, though, and many therefore who desired their freedom fled to parts of the United States like Michigan, Ohio, and New York where slavery was on the decline. The United States Congress in 1787 had passed the Northwest Ordinance banning slavery in its territory north of the Ohio River.

What Simcoe's limited anti-slavery measure did was to set the stage for the influx of thousands of escapees from the American South. Soon after the War of 1812, secret routes were being used by the enslaved to make their way to the North and Canada. Many of these routes were old First Nations' pathways or military trails. Gradually a more organized system of assisting freedom seekers evolved. This became known as the "Underground Railroad." At the peak of its activity in the 1850s, this "railroad" consisted of half a dozen major routes and numerous secondary routes leading from the southern United States to Canada, Mexico, and the Caribbean. At least half of those who reached

Canada West (the name Upper Canada was given after 1840) travelled alone, however, or reached the border with only the chance kindness of strangers to assist them.

The Underground Railroad was not a real railroad. The term referred to the system of secret routes and safe houses by which enslaved "fugitives" made their way to freedom. Wilbur Siebert in *The Underground Railroad from Slavery to Freedom* tells us that the term may have originated in 1831 when a man enslaved in Kentucky, Tice Davids, escaped across the Ohio River and disappeared from view. Davids's owner, who had been in hot pursuit, watched as his human "property" swam across the river. Once the enslaved man reached the opposite shore, however, he could not be found. After a lengthy search, Davids's owner remarked, "The ... Abolitionists must have a Rail-road under the ground."[1]

Because steam locomotion was a new form of transportation, the name "Underground Railroad" caught on and was used by abolitionists as a metaphor to describe their activities in assisting escaping enslaved persons. This railroad terminology included "stations" or "stops," houses in which sympathizers took in fugitives temporarily; "stationmasters," or the selfless people who took them in, and "conductors" who risked their own lives and liberty in transporting runaways from one point to the next. "Cargo" was the human "freight" that risked all for their very freedom.

The Underground Railroad involved many people of good will, all willing to take risks, including Indigenous people and both Blacks and whites. These courageous individuals provided shelter, food, clothing, and secrecy to assist the refugees. Sometimes "conductors" drove wagons, carriages, or carts with people hidden in false compartments. At other times, freedom seekers were disguised as enslaved men driving the carriages of their "owners," who were, in reality, Underground Railroad workers. Sometimes such refugees were dressed in fancy clothing, women dressed up as men and men as women, and those who were light-skinned pretended to be white people or even slave owners. Husband and wife William and Ellen Craft were able to win their freedom by disguising themselves

Harriet Tubman (1822–1913), photographed about 1871–76 by Harvey B. Lindsley. Tubman was the enslaved Maryland fugitive who first emancipated herself and then led dozens to freedom on the Underground Railroad. Known as the "Moses of Her People," she served the Union Army as a nurse, scout, and spy during the Civil War.

as slave and master because Ellen had light skin and she put on male clothing. There were numerous cases of freedom seekers hiding in crates and being shipped north by rail. Henry "Box" Brown acquired his nickname as a result of having escaped this way. He would spend the latter part of his life in Toronto, living close to the Blackburn home just west of the Don River. A number of people risked their lives by making trips into the South to snatch their loved ones from the jaws of slavery.

Perhaps the best-known Underground Railroad "conductor" was Harriet Tubman. This incredible woman is believed to have returned thirteen times to the southern states, where slavery was a part of everyday life, to rescue dozens of bondspeople.[2] Harriet Tubman had herself fled Maryland slavery. From 1851 to 1857, she made St. Catharines, Canada West,[3] her base of operations. "The Moses of Her People" was never caught and was able to bring her brothers and aged parents to St. Catharines with her. As Harriet once exclaimed, "I never ran my train off the track, and I never lost a passenger." She sometimes visited Reverend Michael Willis, president of both Toronto's Knox

Harriet Shephard escaping Maryland slavery, with her five children and five other freedom seekers, using her enslaver's carriages and horses. From William Still's *The Underground Rail Road*.

College and of the Anti-Slavery Society of Canada. He provided some of the funding for her dangerous journeys.

African Americans had been coming to Canada for decades, but it was the passage in the U.S. of the dreaded Fugitive Slave Act of 1850 that sent many thousands more fleeing across the border. This Act strengthened a federal law first passed in 1793. It required officials to arrest and detain any person suspected of being a runaway and rewarded those who returned such people to the slaveholders who claimed to own them. Free Blacks as well as those who had fled slavery years earlier were sometimes kidnapped and sent into slavery. As a result, thousands of African Americans living in freedom in the northern American states packed up and moved to Canada. In effect, no Black person living in the United States, enslaved or free, was safe from the slave catchers after the passage of this law.

The vast majority of freedom seekers were men — about 80 percent. It was far more difficult for women who were pregnant or who had families of young children to make the dangerous trip north. At first, refugees from bondage came on foot, by boat, or in covered wagons, stagecoaches, and carriages. By the 1850s, they also took advantage of the new steam trains, sometimes travelling openly in disguise, and at other times in hidden compartments.

Escape by boat was one of the earliest and most widely used methods of entry, particularly for those living near the coast or along inland rivers. However, once they reached the Canadian border every freedom seeker had to cross the waters of either the Niagara or Detroit Rivers or one of the Great Lakes, and for that they generally needed assistance. On the Great Lakes the boat service was extensive. Friendly captains of schooners and steamers leaving port cities such as Racine (Wisconsin); Chicago (Illinois); Detroit (Michigan); Sandusky, Cleveland, and Toledo (Ohio); and Buffalo or Rochester (New York) dropped off freedom seekers at ports in Canada West such as Windsor, Amherstburg, Owen Sound, Collingwood, Niagara Falls, Port Dalhousie (which is now part of St. Catharines), Hamilton, Toronto, and Kingston. Blacks could remain in these towns or move further inland.

Some came to Toronto by reaching Montreal or Kingston first, either through the St. Lawrence River route or overland via the New England states or upstate New York. From there, Toronto was only a relatively short boat trip away. Another common route was along the eastern seaboard of the United States, through the Niagara Region and across Lake Ontario to Toronto. Steamers and stagecoaches arrived and departed daily to and from Toronto, and many freedom seekers took the opportunity to use them. Regular travel by rail within Canada West did not begin until 1853 when the first railroad line was built between Toronto and Lake Simcoe. But, as more railways were built, refugees could then escape into Canada by train from multiple departure points in the United States.

The American Civil War fought between 1861 and 1865 put an end to slavery. The Thirteenth Amendment to the U.S. Constitution was passed January 31, 1865, and was ratified on December 5 of the same year. This finally freed all still-enslaved African Americans. Travel on the Underground Railroad halted. Some four million African Americans were liberated of their shackles and forged new lives in freedom. However, at least thirty to forty thousand people who took their passage on the Underground Railroad to Canada had paved the way for their brothers and sisters in the United States.

*City of Detroit, Michigan, 1837, Taken from the Canada Shore Near the Ferry.* William J. Bennett, artist. This was one of the important places where freedom seekers crossed into Canada at what is now Windsor, Ontario.

## WANZER AND GRIGSBY COUPLES' ESCAPE

Two couples who made a trip on the Underground Railroad were immortalized in the classic work *The Underground Rail Road*, written by African American abolitionist William Still in 1872. According to Still, Frank Wanzer and Emily Foster (alias Robert Scott and Ann Wood) and Barnaby and Mary Elizabeth Grigsby (alias John and Mary Boyer) escaped from Virginia on Christmas Eve, 1855, in a carriage owned by their enslavers. Two other men were attempting to escape with them on horseback. The group left during the Christmas holiday because that would give them a couple of days extra time before anyone would realize they were missing.

After travelling for a hundred miles or so they were met by six white men and a boy who demanded to know where they were going. Realizing that they were runaways, the white men ordered them to surrender. It was at this point that both the Black men and the women drew guns and knives and stood their ground. "Shoot! Shoot!! Shoot!!!" exclaimed one of the women, a pistol in one hand and a long dagger in the other, fiery determination in her eyes. When the would-be slave catchers realized that they might not make it out alive, they moved aside and let the couples go on their way. The white posse did, however, manage to capture the two men on horseback.

Frank Wanzer, Emily Foster, and Barnaby and Mary Elizabeth Grigsby making their bid for freedom.

All of the freedom seekers were young — in their early twenties. The two women were sisters from the same plantation. Frank Wanzer and Barnaby Grigsby were enslaved on nearby farms.

The two couples made it to Philadelphia, in the free state of Pennsylvania. There they were taken in and cared for by members of the Philadelphia Vigilance Committee. This was one of many groups of Underground Railroad activists that assisted freedom seekers in eluding the slave catchers. After recuperating in Philadelphia, the couples were sent on to Syracuse, New York, and the Underground Railroad "stationmaster" Jermain Loguen, a Black minister there.

Frank Wanzer and Emily Foster, who were engaged, decided to tie the knot. Reverend Loguen performed the marriage ceremony. From Syracuse the couples went on to Toronto. Mrs. Agnes Willis, wife of the Reverend Michael Willis, who helped Harriet Tubman raise money for her journeys south, was the treasurer of the Toronto Ladies' Association for the Relief of Destitute Colored Fugitives. Mrs. Willis met with the couples and assisted them in obtaining employment. She wrote a letter back to William Still of the Philadelphia Vigilance Committee, as follows:

Portrait of William Still engraved by John Sartain of Philadelphia, 1872.

Toronto, 28th January, Monday evening, 1856

Mr. Still, Dear Sir: —
... They are all of them in pretty good spirits, and I have no doubt they will succeed in whatever business they take up. In the mean time the men are chopping wood and the ladies are getting plenty sewing. We are always glad to see our colored refugees safe here. I remain, dear sir, yours respectfully,

Agnes Willis
Treasurer to the Ladies' Society to aid colored refugees.

British Methodist Episcopal (BME) Church, 1953, formerly on Chestnut Street on what is now the site of the new Ontario Courthouse between Dundas and Armoury Streets.

# four

# SOCIAL, CULTURAL, AND RELIGIOUS LIFE IN TORONTO'S BLACK COMMUNITY

AFRICAN TORONTONIANS WERE instrumental in establishing some of the earliest social, cultural, and religious institutions in the city. Reform societies, educational associations, early personal insurance organizations, and those groups devoted to helping freedom seekers and the poor of the city proliferated. The Society for the Protection of Refugees, the Ladies Colored Fugitive Association, the Queen Victoria Benevolent Society (QVBS), and the Ladies Freedman's Aid Society were all founded by the Black women living in the city.

Ellen Toyer Abbott led the Queen Victoria Benevolent Society (QVBS). She was the wife of Wilson Ruffin Abbott, a very wealthy Black Torontonian, and mother of the first Black medical doctor to be born in Canada, Anderson Ruffin Abbott. The QVBS provided assistance to women in need, and helped newcomers with acquiring an education, settling into the city, healthcare, and burial

*Toronto, Canada West, from the Top of the Jail, 1854.* Edwin Whitefield, artist.

requirements. The Ladies Colored Fugitive Association assisted newly arrived freedom seekers in finding housing, jobs, and generally establishing themselves in the city. The Anti-Slavery Society of Canada also operated an employment office on King Street during the 1850s, to help connect incoming African Americans with potential Toronto employers. Shoemaker and community spokesperson Francis Griffin Simpson was in charge of this employment office for a time.

Black Torontonians founded some of the earliest churches in the city. The First Baptist Church has the distinction of being Toronto's oldest Black institution. Tradition has it that the settlement's very first Baptist assembly began in 1826 when fifteen freedom seekers met in worship on the shores of Lake Ontario. After meetings had been held in various locations about the town, in 1841 monies were raised for the construction of "First Colored Calvinistic Baptist Church." It was built on land purchased from John McGill at the northeast corner of Queen and

Victoria Streets. Reverend Washington Christian pastored the congregation. This church emerged as a leading centre of Black abolitionist activity. It sponsored antislavery lectures and provided shelter, food, clothing, money, and other forms of assistance to newcomers. In later years, additional Baptist congregations arose, one worshipping on the west side of Terauley (Bay) Street between Louisa and Edward Streets. A second is listed in the 1864 city directory as worshipping on the north side of Richmond between York and Bay

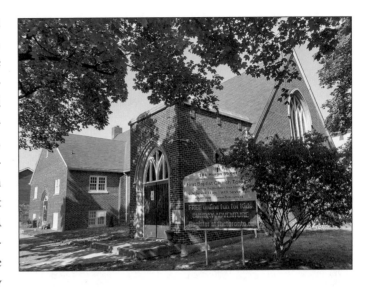

Streets. This was likely a building originally used by a Black Wesleyan Methodist congregation off and on since the 1830s. Today's First Baptist Church is located on Huron Street, north of Dundas.

The land for the present First Baptist Chapel, on the corner of Huron and D'Arcy Streets, was purchased in 1955. From 1841 to 1905, the congregation worshipped in the First Baptist Church on the northeast corner of Victoria and Queen Streets.

African Torontonians established a nondenominational chapel on the north side of Richmond Street west of Bay in about 1830. The minister was Reverend Samuel Brown, who pastored in later years in the Queen's Bush. The next African Canadian church here served a British Wesleyan Congregation. At first, Black Methodists in Toronto had worshipped with whites, but withdrew because they objected to the way they were treated by the white congregations. Canadian Methodist churches also "fellowshipped" with churches that had slaveholding ministers and congregants in the American South. So Black Wesleyans under the leadership of Wilson Ruffin Abbott, and with other trustees, purchased property in 1838 on the north side of Richmond Street between Bay and York. This same building was used for African Methodist Episcopal services until an AME Church could be built on Sayre (Chestnut) Street. The land for the Chestnut Street church was purchased January 31, 1845.

The Coloured Wesleyan Methodist Church formerly at Richmond and York Streets, April 1913. It also served as an African Methodist Episcopal Church (AME) at one time.

The African Methodist Episcopal Church (AME) on Sayre Street was an important focus of Black Toronto life. In 1856, some AME churches broke off from their parent body in the United States and founded a separate denomination that was entirely Canadian in character, the British Methodist Episcopal Church (BME). In part this was due to the fact that the Fugitive Slave Law passed in 1850 prevented Canadian-based AME ministers from attending church conferences south of the border. Those members who wished to continue in the AME tradition met in an old frame schoolhouse at the corner of Terauley (Bay) and Edward Streets through the 1850s, when the congregation joined a new congregation forming on Elm Street.

These and other churches serving the Black community were led by able and highly dedicated ministers, including the charismatic Reverend Washington Christian. In his day, he was noted for establishing more Baptist churches than any other preacher in Canada. Another minister, Reverend William M. Mitchell, had been an active Underground Railroad worker in Ohio before coming to lead the Terauley (Bay) Street Baptist congregation. He travelled to Britain in 1859 to raise money for the construction of a church and wrote a book describing the activities of African American immigrants in Canada. Robert M. Johnson of Indiana came to the city in 1854 as a minister for the AME church and was an active member of the Toronto Literary Society.

The churches served as the centres of benevolent, intellectual, and political life in the community. Antislavery speakers, including the famous formerly enslaved African American Frederick Douglass, British abolitionist George Thompson, and Boston-born Unitarian minister and antislavery activist Reverend Samuel J. May, all delivered addresses from the pulpits of Toronto's Baptist, AME, BME, and Coloured Wesleyan Methodist churches. Charitable activities, including those for the benefit of the ever-increasing numbers of freedom seekers arriving in the provinces, also operated from the church buildings. Activist ministers such as William P. Newman, himself an escaped slave who had been educated at Oberlin College in Ohio, one of very few American universities that accepted African American students, spent several years working between U.S. and Canadian congregations. He also was engaged in a series of colonization schemes to encourage Black Canadians to settle in the Caribbean. Although there was a series of such efforts, most African American immigrants to Toronto stayed in Canada West.

## EMANCIPATION DAY IN TORONTO

Black Canadians played a leading role in the annual Emancipation Day celebrations held in the city on August first. This event commemorated the Emancipation Act of 1833, which ended slavery throughout most of the British slaveholding world, most notably the West Indies and Canada. For African Torontonians this was the most important social happening of the year. They began celebrating Emancipation Day on August 1, 1834. The day was marked by church services, picnics, marches, and parades.

Jehu Jones, a Lutheran minister from Philadelphia, visited Toronto in 1839 and both witnessed and participated in an Emancipation Day celebration. Reverend Jones wrote to New York newspaper editor Charles B. Ray informing Ray that the Toronto Abolition Society, a Black antislavery group, had organized that year's celebrations. It was this group that had extended an invitation to Jones.

Jones revealed that he first attended a church service at the African Methodist Episcopal chapel, at the time located on the north side of Richmond between Bay and York Streets, where Reverend Edward Miller delivered a sermon. From the chapel the celebrants joined a procession that marched to City Hall. Here, city luminaries, such as the mayor, and antislavery leaders, like Reverend H.J. Grasett of the Anglican Church, gave speeches. Afterward, the procession continued to the Commercial Hotel on Front Street, where participants "sat down to a superb dinner." More speeches were made and speakers toasted Queen Victoria and the Royal Family, praising them for their benevolence in abolishing slavery. The British flag flew everywhere. Jones ended the day at a tea party organized "by the ladies of Toronto" in honour of Emancipation Day. Jones also commented that the parade was well-organized and controlled by Black marshals. The event was attended by Black and white, young and old, and he noted the co-operation across all levels of Black society, the various cultural institutions, and the different religious denominations.

One of Dr. Anderson Ruffin Abbott's first memories was the Emancipation Day celebration held in 1844. He, too, recorded his observations:

> They provided a banquet which was held under a pavilion erected on a vacant lot running from Elizabeth Street to Sayre Street opposite Osgoode Hall, which was then a barracks for the 92nd West India Regiment. The procession was headed by the band of the Regiment. The tallest man in this Regiment was a Black man, a drummer, known as Black Charlie. The procession carried a Union Jack and a silk blue banner on which was inscribed in gilt letters "The Abolition Society, Organized 1833." The mayor of the city, Mr. Metcalfe, made a speech ... followed by several other speeches of prominent citizens. These celebrations were carried on yearly amid much enthusiasm.

On March 24, 2021, the Parliament of Canada voted unanimously to designate Emancipation Day a national event.

Emancipation Day Parade, Amherstburg, Ontario, 1890s.

Toronto from the top of the Rossin House Hotel at King and York Streets looking north, 1856. Just right of the middle foreground is a woman on her porch. The image is believed to be the earliest Toronto photo of an African Canadian woman.

# five

# LIFE IN THE CITY

TORONTO IN THE MID-1800s was a "walking" city. People lived near the places where they worked, close to the churches they attended, and, if possible, near enough to a public school for their children to gain an education. The oldest Black families in the city operated businesses in what had once been the old Town of York, east of Yonge and south of King Street near St. Lawrence Market and the steamboat docks at the foot of Church Street. Several had homes and businesses on Church, as well.

Others moved to newly opened up parts of the city west of Yonge. A number of free Black families from Richmond, Virginia, migrated to the city in the early 1830s. The Hickmans, Gallegos, and four Edmunds brothers, all barbers by trade, arrived in the wake of the Nat Turner Slave Rebellion of 1831 and its bloody aftermath. The Virginia legislature had reacted by passing harsh new laws prohibiting education for Black people and requiring all those who were free to leave the state within a year or risk re-enslavement. Such newcomers to Toronto

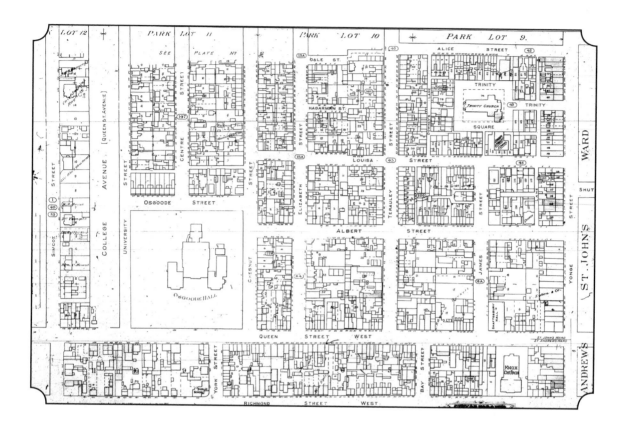

Fire insurance map of St. John's Ward, where many of Toronto's recent African American immigrants lived. From Goad's *Atlas of the City of Toronto*, 1884.

brought both skills and the money to purchase real estate. Several settled on York Street between Richmond and Lot (Queen) Streets.

On arrival, the formerly enslaved as well as free Black immigrants often boarded north of this district, staying with families in the area that was originally part of St. Patrick's Ward, but subdivided from it in 1852 when St. John's Ward was created. The area lay north of Queen Street and was bounded on the west by University Avenue and on the east by Yonge Street. Although the city did not have a defined Black neighbourhood, St. John's Ward was a favourite place of residence for many immigrant families, Black and white. Some streets, such as Centre Street, which ran north from behind Osgoode Hall as far as present-day College Street, had substantial African American refugee populations. The north end of the street was home to several formerly enslaved families originally from Baltimore, Maryland.

William Still, secretary of the Philadelphia Vigilance Committee and himself the son of formerly enslaved parents, assisted hundreds of refugees on their way to the northern states and Canada. He recorded the stories of many who later made Toronto their home.

James Burrell, who fled from Virginia, sent a letter to Still once he arrived. He wrote in 1854 that he was boarding with Robert Phillips, who lived on the west side of Centre Street behind Osgoode Hall. Two years later, James Monroe, Peter Heines, Henry James Morris, and Matthew Bodams, all from North Carolina, informed Still that they were sharing rented rooms at Mr. George Blount's, just up the street from the Phillips' home. Many other African American immigrants lived on adjacent streets such as Elizabeth, Agnes (Dundas), Terauley (Bay), and Albert, several of which disappeared in the redevelopment for the "new" City Hall and the Toronto Eaton Centre block. Others owned businesses further west along Bathurst, Queen, and Portland Streets, and eastward in the area of St. Lawrence Market and along Church Street.

New immigrants, Black and white, could afford to live in the modest one- and two-storey wooden houses lining the narrow streets of St. John's Ward and what remained of the old St. Patrick's Ward, which at the time ran north of Queen and west of University Avenue to about the modern line of Ossington. A very dynamic Black community grew up in the district. Education was a priority; in Toronto, public schools provided free education without regard to skin colour. At the end of a long working week, the children's parents and grandparents learned to read and write in the Sabbath Schools run by three local African Canadian churches.

African American immigrants possessed skills and abilities that gave them a head start in their new land. By 1850, Black Torontonians owned homes and businesses in several parts of town. Wilson Ruffin Abbott, who had arrived in 1835 and originally worked as a tobacconist, was the wealthiest member of the

The building at 94 Albert Street was owned and occupied by Wilson Ruffin Abbott in the 1850s.

community. His real estate holdings extended as far north as Owen Sound. John M. Tinsley was also very successful, and regularly employed newly arrived refugees from bondage in his carpentry business on Agnes (Dundas) Street, just west of Bay. Skilled cooks owned restaurants and taverns that also provided jobs: the Tontine Coffee House was operated by Daniel Bloxom at 150 King Street East and the popular Epicurean Recess Restaurant at Church and Colborne was the property of Beverly Randolph Snow. He had fled Washington, D.C., in the summer of 1835 when his gourmet restaurant, the Epicurean Eating House on Pennsylvania Avenue, was burned to the ground at the centre of a racist outbreak. "The Snow Riots," as they came to be known, destroyed many Black homes and institutions.

As more and more freedom seekers reached Toronto, the city gained a number of blacksmiths, including Charles Peyton Lucas, formerly of Leesburg, Virginia; bricklayers; carpenters; and masons. Women earned their livings as washerwomen, seamstresses, hairdressers, or milliners (hat- and bonnet-makers). Mrs. Mary O. Augusta, wife of one of the city's two to three Black doctors, had a successful ladies accessory store on York Street, later moving to larger premises on Yonge. In 1833, Willis Addison was listed as operating a small grocery on York between Adelaide and Richmond, while in later years he was employed as a plasterer living at Bathurst and Queen. Matthew Truss, a shoemaker, had his own shop on Queen near Church and, interestingly, lived with his family in the old Russell Abbey on Front Street, where the Pompadour family had been enslaved by Peter Russell and his sister years earlier. Mrs. Frances Teackle, a widow, was a candy maker who lived on Centre Street north of Osgoode Hall. She owned two confectionery shops in the city. Barber William Hickman's wife, Betsey, ran the family grocery store on York Street, while by the 1870s Adolphus Judah's son Phillip and his wife, Caroline Judah, were operating a fine fruit and vegetable shop at the northwest corner of Queen and Beverley Streets. The building that housed their store is still standing.

Still other formerly enslaved people had worked in service, and thus gained a variety of skills that could be turned into gainful employment, such as barbering, operating a tobacco shop, or doing fancy ironing. Some men, like Benjamin Pollard Holmes, worked on ships that plied the Great Lakes, while others were employed as waiters in the fine dining rooms of Toronto's luxury hotels or, seasonally, at resort hotels on both sides of the border at Niagara Falls. Widows sometimes operated boarding houses or rented out flats or houses to support their children. In a large city like Toronto there was always employment for those with fewer skills — labourers and dockworkers, draymen and porters, and housekeepers or charwomen who cleaned people's homes for a living.

Advertisement in the *Provincial Freeman*, October 28, 1854, for Mrs. Augusta's fancy dress shop.

Bloor Street West in the late 1800s.

# six

# LIVING ON THE OUTSKIRTS

SOME AFRICAN AMERICAN IMMIGRANTS settled in the downtown core, while others headed to the outskirts of the city. In fact, the Township of York held the second-highest population of Blacks outside of St. John's Ward in Toronto proper. In 1861, York Township was a large area of land surrounding the City of Toronto. It was bounded by the Humber River and Etobicoke Township on the west, Scarborough Township on the east, Markham and Vaughan Townships to the north, and Lake Ontario and the city limits at Bloor Street on the south. Yonge Street separated York Township East from York Township West.

What attracted immigrants to the fringes of the urban world? As was the case with many African American migrants, these settlers were drawn to a rural environment more like the one they had known in the United States. Some farmed, while other families were attracted by the cheaper land prices, lower taxes, and the greater availability of good-sized lots for gardening, keeping a cow, a couple of pigs, or some chickens. Being close to the city provided ready markets for those

Davenport Railway Station on the west side of Caledonia Park Road north of Davenport Road, 1863.

engaged in market gardening, who would bring their produce by wagon south down Yonge Street, swinging west to avoid its muddiest parts, past the tollbooth at Davenport near Bathurst, and then east again down to St. Lawrence Market.

Many of the men were labourers, who performed such tasks as clearing land, chopping wood, hauling goods by horse and cart, building barns and houses, and doing seasonal farm work. Women also worked in the fields as market gardeners or brought other people's laundry into their own homes as washerwomen. A few worked as servants in private households, or did housekeeping, were chamber maids, or cooked in saloons and hotels. Married women and widows also earned money by taking in boarders, usually single men.

In 1861, many families of note lived in Ward 3 of York Township West, where Deborah Brown made her home. In this particular district, near what today is the corner of Bathurst and Bloor Streets, lived the highest number of African Canadians and African American immigrants found in all of York Township. Well-known Underground Railroad refugees the Wanzers and Grigsbys were two families living there. The couples shared a one-storey frame house on the lot next to that of Deborah and Perry Brown. Frank and Emily Wanzer were thirty and twenty-eight years of age respectively, and Barnaby and Mary Grigsby were thirty-three and thirty respectively, according to the census-taker. The Wanzers owned a horse and four pigs, all valued at $15, and the couples lived on one-half acre of land. The two men were labourers and both couples worshipped in the Wesleyan Methodist faith.

The Wanzers had two additions to their family by 1861. Two-year-old Mary Wanzer and one-year-old George had both been born in Canada. The Grigsby family did not have any children.

Another neighbour of Deborah Brown was Reverend William M. Mitchell, his wife,

Pioneer Hotel in Seaton Village at the corner of Bathurst and Bloor Streets, circa 1890. This building was a couple of blocks from the house of Deborah Brown.

Elizabeth, and their five children. Reverend Mitchell was a Baptist minister and abolitionist who was active in the African Canadian community of Toronto. The Mitchell family lived in a one-storey frame house on a three-quarter-acre plot of land. At the time the 1861 census was taken, the Reverend was in England speaking on behalf of the African community in Canada and raising funds for his church. He preached at the Coloured Regular Baptist Church in St. John's Ward, in downtown Toronto.

Reverend Mitchell may have obtained a ride to the church each Sunday with the Richards family in their horse-drawn buggy. Richard B. Richards was a respected member and trustee of the Coloured Regular Baptist Church. He and his family would have attended the downtown church on a regular basis.

Enhancing his stature among Black Baptists, Richard B. Richards owned a successful ice business and lived on a three-acre farm on Davenport Road in Ward 3. In addition to his wife, Sarah, and their three grown children, Richards' brothers and brother-in-law and their families lived on the property. Richards' daughters Harriet, aged twenty-six, and Nancy, aged twenty-five, worked as a tailoress and dressmaker, respectively. His son, William, aged twenty-two, was a grocer by trade.

George Washington Carter, most likely the Richards' son-in law, was a barber living with his wife and four-year-old daughter. Henry Richards, another brother, was a labourer and widower with four children aged eleven to twenty-one.

These families represent the different levels of social and economic status that Black people had attained in the province. Often, the length of time a family had been in Canada determined how well its members succeeded in their new environment and how much property they were able to acquire. This was true of all new immigrants to the province.

## JEFFERSON AND MARY PIPKINS

One of the heart-wrenching aspects of escape on the Underground Railroad, as has been seen, was the fact that children often had to be left behind. Jefferson and Mary L. Pipkins (or Pipkin) were also neighbours of Deborah Brown and her husband. The Pipkins had escaped from Baltimore, Maryland, in April 1853, and found their way to the Philadelphia Vigilance Committee. With the help of the antislavery network in Philadelphia and New York, the Pipkins ultimately settled in York Township West near the Browns, the Wanzers, and the Grigsbys. Several years after their escape, as the following letter from Jefferson Pipkins illustrates, the couple was still trying to find a way out of slavery for their four children:

Sept. 28, 1856.

To Wm. Still. Sir:

I take the liberty of writing to you a few lines concerning my children, for I am anxious to get them and I wish you to please try what you can do for me. Their names are Charles and Patrick and are living with Mrs. Joseph G. Wray Murphysborough Hartford county, North Carolina; Emma lives with a lawyer Baker in Gatesville North Carolina and Susan lives in Portsmouth Virginia and is stopping with Dr. Collins sister a Mrs. Nash ... And I trust you will try what you think will be the best way. And you will do me a great favor. Yours Respectfully,

Jefferson Pipkins.
P.S. I am living at Yorkville near Toronto Canada West. My wife sends her best respects to Mrs. Still.

William Still, of the Philadelphia Vigilance Committee, noted that, sadly, nothing could be done by the committee to abduct relatives still in slavery because it was simply too dangerous. By 1861, it is known that Mr. and Mrs. Pipkins were still living in York Township West and that none of their children were living with them in the household. Jefferson Pipkins, aged sixty, was employed as a labourer and his wife, Mary, was reported to be forty-eight years of age and, as was usually the case for wives, had no employment listed beside her name in the census.

Did the couple ever see their children again? Incredibly, one child may have joined her mother after Emancipation. By 1871, Jefferson Pipkins had died. An Emma Pipkins is listed as living with Mary Pipkins in both the 1871 and 1881 census for York Township. Could this be the Emma mentioned as living in slavery in North Carolina? The Emma named in the 1871 census was reported as having been born in Ontario and was now ten years old. She was also reported to be "English," as compared with Mary Pipkins's designation as "African." She appeared again with Mary Pipkins in the 1881 census, and this time neither was listed as "African." These discrepancies probably reflect the ignorance of the census taker, who may have mistaken light skin

Census of Canada, 1871, York Township West, Division 4. Mary and Emma Pipkins (spelled Pipkin) are listed as shown. Two households above them are Mr. and Mrs. Wanzer and their children Mary and Abigail. By 1871, the Grigsbys had moved to St. John's Ward and were joined by Smith W. Grigsby, aged 50. Could he have been Barnaby Grigsby's father, who made the trek north to live with his son after emancipation from slavery in the United States?

for whiteness. Interestingly, in contrast to the 1861 and 1871 census records, in which no occupation was given, in 1881 Emma was described as a dressmaker, while Mary Pipkins was described as a laundress.

In 1871, Mary Pipkins was sixty-three years of age. She was perhaps too old to be the child's mother. Could Emma have been her grandchild? It is entirely possible that Mary Pipkins had reunited with one or more of her children and that she was raising one of her grandchildren. Her children may simply have been living in a separate household elsewhere. Although we may never be able to solve this mystery, it would certainly be nice to speculate that Mary Pipkins reunited with at least one of her children. She died in 1888 in Newmarket, Ontario, and was buried beside her husband in the Toronto Necropolis.

In addition to the Black community of York Township, there were smaller numbers of people of African descent living in places surrounding Toronto, such as Scarborough, Markham, Vaughan, King, and Etobicoke. To the west of York Township, Etobicoke Township had the second largest community of Blacks, although the numbers were much smaller than in York Township. In 1861, on the eve of the American Civil War, there were eighty-three people of African descent living in Etobicoke.

Toronto historian Hilary Dawson has studied Joshua Glover, who settled in Etobicoke. Glover escaped from his owner in St. Louis, Missouri, in the spring of 1850. He found his way to Racine, Wisconsin, later that summer and promptly found a job at a lumber mill just outside of town. Glover was enjoying a life in relative freedom, but this was not to last. His owner, Benammi S. Garland, discovered his whereabouts and determined to snatch his "property" back.

On March 10, 1854, Garland and an armed posse of four men including a St. Louis policeman, a U.S. marshal, a deputy marshal, and a notorious slave catcher from a nearby town went to Joshua's home and knocked on his door. When the door opened, the men rushed in. Glover tried to bat Garland's pistol away, but the marshal dealt Glover a sharp blow to the head with his handcuffs. The deputy marshal then struck him with the butt end of his whip. Glover hit the floor and was carried to a wagon, a severe wound on his head gushing blood. Garland started off for Milwaukee with his captive, arriving about three in the morning to the county jail there.

In the meantime, antislavery forces got wind of Glover's capture. They began to amass a large crowd to oppose what they considered to be his "kidnapping." About five o'clock that afternoon a large crowd of people opposed to slavery started to ram the doors of the jail and eventually breached them. Glover emerged and waved his hat to the crowd. He hopped into a two-horse wagon that scurried down to the Milwaukee River and crossed to the other side. Glover was then transferred to a lighter buggy and was whisked away. He remained in Wisconsin for several weeks, moving from safe house to safe house to evade the slave catchers.

Bronze and black galaxy stone bust, erected in the Joshua Glover Park at 4208 Dundas Street West, overlooking the Humber River valley. Quentin VerCetty, artist.

He even spent time back in Racine, as it was rightly believed that the enemy would not suspect him there. After about five weeks of hiding out, Glover was transported by one of the Great Lakes ships to Canada West (Ontario). Many ship captains at this time were willing to hide and transport fugitive slaves to Canadian ports, and Glover was one of them.

By April 19, 1854, Glover had arrived in Etobicoke. How do we know this? The account book of Thomas Montgomery, owner of Montgomery's Inn and a large landowner in the area, gives us the answer. Montgomery wrote in his account book that he had given "Joshua Glover the Negro" 15 shillings, or about $3.00, as an advance on wages. This was the first of many notations in the account book dealing with Joshua Glover. Glover did farm work for Montgomery, such as chopping wood and harvesting crops. He also rented from Montgomery a small one-storey cabin with a cookstove for $2 a month. It was located near the Humber River. Other African Americans turned African Canadians mentioned by Montgomery were carpenters John Dunkins (or Duncan) and John Winston Skanks. Skanks built fences, gates, and a porch for Montgomery.

The April 1854 transaction regarding Joshua Glover recorded in Thomas Montgomery's account book was the beginning of a relationship with the Montgomery family that lasted for over thirty years. Joshua Glover's story is told in *Finding Freedom: The Untold Story of Joshua Glover, Runaway Slave* by Ruby West Jackson and Walter T. McDonald. Montgomery's Inn, at the corner of Islington Avenue and Dundas Street West, is now a Toronto historic site and museum.

## SUSANNAH STOKES MAXWELL: RICHMOND HILL

In 1923, Richmond Hill resident Susannah Stokes Maxwell passed away. She was 117 years old. At the time of her passing she was known as "Canada's oldest citizen." Maxwell was a Black Canadian woman who had lived in Richmond Hill for over fifty years. She exemplifies the long history of African Canadians in Richmond Hill, a town just north of Toronto.

Susannah was born in 1805 to free Black parents in Lancaster County, Pennsylvania. She grew up and married Henry Maxwell. They built a life for themselves in the village of Christiana. Eventually they had five children. Christiana became a destination for African Americans who had fled slavery in the Deep South.

In 1851, the village was attacked by slave catchers and slave owners in search of their prey. Many of the formerly enslaved people living there fought back and one of the slave catchers, Edward Gorsuch, was killed. In the aftermath, Susannah and Henry fled to New York State. From New York, in 1855, they travelled to Toronto. There Susannah worked as a laundress and Henry as a coal burner. Seeking better opportunities north of Toronto in Richmond Hill, in 1871 the Maxwells moved there.

In their new home, Susannah opened a laundry, assisted by her daughters Mary and Tillie. Census reports for Richmond Hill reveal that Susannah attended both the local Methodist and Presbyterian churches. In fact, the Maxwell home was located just across Yonge Street from the latter.

On her one hundredth birthday, in 1905, the citizens of Richmond Hill and surrounding areas celebrated Susannah at the Presbyterian church. A local judge, William Glenholme Falconbridge, gave her a gift of $75. Susannah was an active participant in the development of Richmond Hill and surrounding region.

Bathurst Street looking north from about Lonsmount Drive, 1915.

Northwest of Toronto there were forty-one individuals of African descent living in King Township in 1861. Among them were Benjamin and Sarah (Britton) Rollings who, along with their children, operated the general store on Weston Road at Laskay. Benjamin was the first Black postmaster in Canada. Their son Walter Rollings, born in 1873, would go on to graduate from the Newmarket Normal School (teachers' college). He served for more than forty years as the beloved principal of Kingshorn School, a school with an almost entirely European-Canadian student body.

There were also Black families living to the northeast of Toronto in Markham and surrounding areas. In 1861, census figures show that ten Markham residents were of African descent, although the listing of Black Canadians in official records is very often far lower than the actual population. John Washington, aged thirty-three, and his wife, Charlotte, who was twenty-seven, are listed as living in Markham in the 1871 census. They were both born in the United States, but their three young children — Rossanna, Elizabeth, and George — were all born in Canada. John worked as a labourer, likely in the employ of local German Mennonite farmers such as Emmanuel Doner and his next-door neighbour, seventy-four-year-old David Eger.

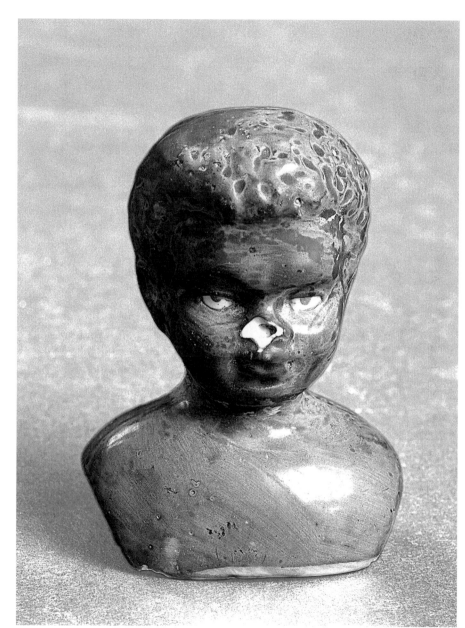

Black porcelain doll's head, made in Germany for the African American market. This may have belonged to the young daughter of barber Edward Jones at 39 Centre Street. Found at the Courthouse Site in St. John's Ward.

# seven

# THE WORLD OF CHILDREN

WHENEVER POSSIBLE, those who escaped slavery brought their children with them to Toronto. Many examples exist of men and women who, once free, desperately tried to purchase or even "steal" their children away from Southern slaveholders. Free people, too, who had formerly lived in the northern United States came to Toronto in family groups throughout the period before the Civil War.

One interesting example was Elizabeth Hudson, her husband, William, and their young ones. Their path from slavery to freedom can be traced through the birthplaces of their four children. Their eldest son, Thomas Henry Hudson, was born in North Carolina, while his parents were still enslaved. By the time Clara Elizabeth was born in 1854, the family had escaped to Connecticut. They moved in the next year even farther away from Southern slave catchers, settling in Boston, where William was born. By 1861, they are recorded as living on Toronto's Centre Street, behind Osgoode Hall, and had a new daughter, Selia, born after their arrival in 1859.

*Sam, the Toronto Shoe-Shine Boy, 1898.* Joshua Biehn, artist. This rare portrait shows a Black boy peeling an orange with a newspaper under his arm, from which hangs a shoeshine kit. While the detail is striking, the work portrays a negative stereotypical image of a Black child in Toronto at the turn of the twentieth century.

Life in early Toronto was difficult for infants and children. Various epidemics swept through the downtown core in the nineteenth century. Cholera is said to have killed one in four Torontonians in 1857. Disease was most deadly in areas of high population concentration, and where outdoor toilets existed side-by-side with public wells. These were common conditions in early Toronto, and children of the rich and poor alike were victims of deadly illness.

Immunization was not yet common and medical care was still primitive. Cemetery records show that many babies died of what today would be minor illnesses: infections and fever were responsible for many infant deaths, as were childhood illnesses like measles, chickenpox, and mumps.

It is particularly poignant to note that the Wanzer family of York Township, who had overcome so much just to reach Canada, lost four youngsters in the space of twelve years. Three died as infants, including little George F. Wanzer who was only a one-year-old when the 1861 census was recorded, and who died half a year later of consumption (tuberculosis). Another infant, Frank, died in 1869 at four months old, of whooping cough; and a third, Nathaniel, in 1870 at three months, eleven days, of teething. This last cause of death may seem particularly shocking, but it was not uncommon in the nineteenth century. The child could have died of a fever associated with teething, or his gums might have been lanced to allow the teeth to come through, causing him to die of infection. Most tragic of all, however, may have been the death of Mary E. Wanzer, at the age of fourteen. She died of an abscess in 1873.

High infant mortality rates were a fact of life. Indeed, many families lived with one or more tragedies of this nature. Reverend Mitchell's daughter Eliza, who had been born in Ohio, died of inflammation in 1861 at the age of six years, eleven months. These untimely deaths also suggest the lack of adequate health care and the absence of qualified medical personnel on the fringes of the urban environment. Many of these children, as well as their parents, were buried in the Toronto Necropolis cemetery. It is located on Winchester Street across from today's Riverdale Farm.

(top) Children's cup and marbles. Found at the Courthouse Site in St. John's Ward.

(bottom) Children's cup and china dog, discovered at the Courthouse Site.

Like all immigrant groups in the nineteenth-century city, many African Canadian families were forced to send their children to work. Very little record exists of the lives of working Black children, but most likely they sold newspapers, were employed as whitewashers, shined shoes, and laboured in the foundries, blacksmith shops, tanneries, and livery stables in early Toronto.

However, a very strong emphasis on education characterized African Canadian society. In most American states before the Civil War, it was against the law to teach an enslaved person to read. This was because slaveholders were afraid that their human "property" would acquire ideas about freedom from what they read, especially if they were reading the Bible or any of the many booklets and articles published by American antislavery groups. They also might be tempted to write for themselves one of the "passes" that slaveholders issued authorizing enslaved African Americans to travel from one place to another. Such a document might permit a freedom seeker to evade capture long enough to cross over into the Northern states. Once they reached Canada, however, the formerly enslaved wanted nothing more than to acquire an education for their children, and also for themselves. Churches operated "Sabbath Schools" and night schools, teaching adults to read alongside their children.

Toronto was unique in nineteenth-century Canada in that the public schools and schools of higher learning were always open to Black students. In most parts of the province, Black immigrants to Canada were forced to found and support private schools, because local officials barred children of colour from the public schools. Parents sent petition after petition to government officials, demanding that schooling be made available, often with little result.

The children of St. John's and St. Patrick's Wards had a choice of several schools. The Toronto Board of Education operated public schools in the downtown core beginning in the middle of the nineteenth century. Census documents list the number of children in each household who were attending school. Louisa Street School, Phoebe Street School, and Richmond Street School were all within a short walk of many African Canadian homes. In the 1861 census, eight-year-old William H. Brown, a member of Deborah Brown's household, was away attending school in the city. He may very well have been the H. Brown boarding with the family of Francis Griffin Simpson, a shoemaker and community spokesperson who lived at 25 Elizabeth Street in St. John's Ward. The best Anglican boys' school, Upper Canada College, had several African Canadian students over the years, beginning in the 1830s with Peter Gallego. He was the brilliant son of Philip Gallego, who had relocated his family from Richmond, Virginia, to York Street in the early 1830s. Intending upon a career as a missionary to Africa, Gallego was sponsored by Reverend John Strachan, the Anglican archdeacon and then bishop of York. Alfred Lafferty, son of a formerly enslaved man who ran a cartage business, and William Henry Smallwood, whose father, Thomas Smallwood, was a master saw-maker and had brought his family to Toronto when his Underground Railroad activities in and around Washington, D.C., were exposed, both enrolled in 1853. William H. Abbott, youngest son of Wilson Ruffin Abbott and Ellen Toyer Abbott, attended Upper Canada College in 1859.

Schoolroom in the Victoria Industrial School, Mimico (now part of Toronto), 1898.

Lafferty's career was stellar. According to Toronto historian Hilary Dawson, "In 1856, Alfred passed the Upper Canada College Annual Examination to win a scholarship — or 'exhibition,' as it was called. His fees (£2.10 a term) were waived for the rest of his stay there. He matriculated with honours in 1859, winning two of the College's four major awards: His Excellency the Governor General's Prize and The Mathematical Prize."

Several Black scholars graduated with honours from Trinity College, University College (where Alfred Lafferty later enrolled), Victoria College (William H. Abbott studied for the ministry there), the Toronto School of Medicine, and, particularly, the Toronto Normal School, which was the teachers' college. Emeline Shadd, sister of noted newspaper publisher, abolitionist, and educator Mary Ann Shadd Cary, won first prize for proficiency in 1855 at the Toronto Normal School. In 1862, she married free-born Reverend Henry Simpson, Francis Griffin Simpson's brother. Emeline spent from 1872 to 1876 teaching the formerly enslaved people of the Sea Islands, Georgia, to read and write. Also a graduate of the Toronto Normal School was James Rapier, who returned to the South during Reconstruction and became the first African American Congressman for Alabama.

Samuel Ringgold Ward was a well-known and eloquent Congregational minister. He came to Canada after participating in the famous rescue of freedom seeker "Jerry" in Syracuse, New York. Ward served as agent for the Anti-Slavery Society of Canada, touring the province and giving speeches. He was an agent for the *Voice of the Fugitive* and also edited the *Provincial Freeman* with Mary Ann Shadd Cary.

## eight

# POLITICAL LIFE

THOUGH BLACKS FOUND a measure of protection and security in Toronto, they faced discrimination and racism in many aspects of their lives. However, they did not simply let this go by. Black Torontonians' response to the minstrel shows illustrates how they fought negative stereotypes and racism.

Starting in the U.S. in the 1830s, profoundly racist "Black" minstrel shows soon became a common form of entertainment. The actors, in fact, were neither Black nor of African heritage, but white people who smeared their faces and bodies with soot or shoe polish, the origin of the term *blackface*. Then, on stage, they would mimic what they believed to be African American behaviour, making fun particularly of those suffering under the harsh and exploitative regime of Southern plantation slavery. White audiences enjoyed these performances. Blacks did not. African Canadians all over the province felt that minstrel shows insulted and demeaned Black people, their way of life, and their culture.

As was true in cities across North America, in Toronto such minstrel shows were frequently performed. In 1840, African Torontonians took a stand against them.

Toronto Minstrel Show at McCormick Playground, January 29, 1920.

Led by Wilson Ruffin Abbott, forty-five members of the Black community signed a petition and went to city hall. They asked the mayor and the council to prohibit the performance of minstrel shows in the city. A vote was taken in council, but unfortunately, the majority did not support Abbott and his fellow protesters. This did not deter them, for two years later they tried again. Pointing out that the shows had already been banned in Kingston, this time they won. The minstrel shows that for so long had disparaged Black people were not performed in Toronto for a few years but would later be revived. Blackface minstrel shows continued as a popular form of entertainment as late as the mid-twentieth century.

Support for African Canadian resistance to minstrelsy was in part based on the fact that, in the City of Toronto, the Black vote was important. Politicians of all political parties wanted Black voters to support them in elections. They knew that, often, African Torontonian voters could determine the outcome of elections.

In January 1848, Wilson Ruffin Abbott became the first African Torontonian to run for city councillor, garnering fifty-nine votes. According to the Toronto *Colonist* of January 14, 1848, this included every eligible Black voter in the ward. Sadly, he was defeated by Robert Britton Denison with 175 votes. W.R. Abbott's name appeared frequently in the press encouraging voters to support the Reform platform. The Toronto *Globe* of July 2, 1861, reported on a large rally held by the city's Black community at Mechanics Hall, where Drs. Augusta and Anderson Ruffin Abbott, along with community spokesperson Francis G. Simpson and others, spoke enthusiastically on behalf of Reformer George Brown.

St. Lawrence Hall as it appeared in 1912. Watercolour by Frederick Victor Poole.

Antislavery or abolitionist activities were central to the political life of Black Toronto. Beginning in the 1830s and continuing for another thirty years, Toronto was a hub of antislavery sentiment. Slavery in the United States was not abolished until after the Civil War, and until the conflict ended Black Torontonians kept up a constant agitation against it. A number of Black antislavery leaders in the city had themselves once been enslaved, and so they had first-hand knowledge.

Many free Blacks from the United States also made the trip and settled in Toronto. They brought funds to purchase real estate and start businesses, along

(top) Kentucky-born Henry Walton Bibb escaped from slavery in 1842. Arriving in Detroit, he joined the abolitionist movement and became one of the most renowned antislavery activists and lecturers of his day. This formal photograph of Bibb, taken in 1849 when he was thirty-four, became the frontispiece for his autobiography, *Narrative of the Life and Adventures of Henry Bibb, an American Slave*, published that year. The book became an instant bestseller and went through three printings in eighteen months.

(bottom) The *Voice of the Fugitive* newspaper was first published in 1851 by Henry and Mary Bibb after they moved to Sandwich, Canada West. It reported on matters of interest to Canada's Black community and was very influential because of its staunch antislavery message. The paper ceased publication with Henry Bibb's death in 1854.

# VOICE OF THE FUGITIVE.

**HENRY BIBB, EDITOR.**       **SANDWICH, C. W., MARCH 26, 1851,**       **VOL. I. NO. 7.**

### VOICE OF THE FUGITIVE.

IS PUBLISHED

EVERY OTHER WEDNESDAY, AT SANDWICH CANADA WEST.

ONE DOLLAR per annum, always in advance. No subscription will be received for a less term than six months.

Advertisements, not exceeding ten lines, inserted four times for one dollar. Every subsequent insertion twenty five cents.

Great Anti-Slavery Meetings at Auburn and Syracuse.

Resolved, That the iniquity of our National Legislature has culminated in the enactment of " the Fugitive Slave Law." It is now, therefore, for the people to decide wether our Republic shall be wholly given up to the despotic misrule of the Southern oligarchy, until it shall be engulphed in that ruin which has always overwhelmed oppressive governments, or wether by a stern refusal to comply with the requisitions of this law, they will compell our legislators to return to the way of righteousness which alone are ways of happy union and enduring peace.

Resolved, That the uprising of " the people" everywhere at the North in op-

you can to deliver them who are not bound out of the hands of the spoiler.

The weapons of our warfare not being carnal, but mighty, through God, to the pulling down of strong holds, we may with certainty calculate upon a glorious triumph, if we battle together in the unity of the Spirit and the bonds of peace, wielding with boldness the sword of the Spirit, which is the word of God :

For Christ and Humanity,

SARAH H. ERNST, Pres't.
M. M. GUILD, Sec'y.
Cincinnatti, Ohio, Feb., 12, 1851.

and the most solemn duty they can be summoned to discharge this side of eternity. If it can be morally right for men, whose breath is in their nostrils, to arrogate to themselves half the prerogative of the Almighty, who can not only kill but make alive, then those who are nearest like him in spirit should be the only ones qualified and selected to discharge this awful duty. Those set apart to kill and be killed, should be parraded with a spirit which could fellowship with the spirit of heaven, and fit them for its society, whilst in the act of stabbing at each others' hearts, or weltering in their gore. If men are to be sent by regiments

### FLAX COTTON.

Whatever may have been the failure of former efforts—and the attempt is by no means a new one—to employ flax as a substitute for cotton, and adapt it to being spun and woven by the ordinary machinery of the cotton mill, we must concede something of possibility to the science and inventive genius of the age which has produced photography and the magnetic telegraph. It is difficult to conceive of any thing inherently impracticable in the undertaking, and the tone of the British papers—we may say the changed tone of some of them, which a short time ago with experience in community organizing, the creation of benevolent and fraternal organizations, and a deep commitment to the antislavery cause. Because of the influx there grew up a number of intellectual associations in the mid-nineteenth-century city, such as the Young Men's Excelsior Literary and Debating Society, which met at the Sayre (now Chestnut) Street BME Church. The president was Francis G. Simpson, formerly of Schenectady, New York.

St. Lawrence Hall on King Street East was constructed after the Great Toronto Fire of 1849 as a cultural, social, and political centre for the city. It was here in February 1851, that an interracial group including two Scots (George Brown, publisher of the *Globe*, and Michael Willis, Principal of Knox College) and Black abolitionists (including publisher Henry Bibb and A.B. Jones, of London, Canada West) founded the Anti-Slavery Society of Canada. Soon after its beginning, the Society invited renowned antislavery British Parliamentarian George Thompson, American Unitarian minister Samuel Joseph May, and eloquent formerly enslaved abolitionist Frederick Douglass himself, to speak at the Hall. They delivered powerful lectures to packed audiences, both there and at churches across the city, and did much to encourage support for the cause.

Perhaps the most important antislavery event to occur in Toronto also took place in 1851. The North American Convention of Coloured People was called and chaired by Henry Walton Bibb, himself a refugee from Southern bondage. He had only been in Canada for about a year. Following the publication of his successful autobiography, Bibb and his wife, Mary Miles Bibb, a schoolteacher and fellow abolitionist, had moved from the United States. Once across the border, he established Canada's first Black newspaper, the *Voice of the Fugitive*, published in Sandwich, near Windsor. This paper championed the cause of Canadian Blacks and called for their full civil rights. The Convention met at St. Lawrence Hall. For three days, more than fifty-three delegates discussed the safety and security of Black people in North America, and ways to improve Black life on the continent. Finally, on the third and final day, Henry Bibb, James Tinsley, and John Fisher each gave an address summing up the sentiments of the delegates on the questions at hand. The delegates concluded that Canada — with Jamaica running second — was the best place for Blacks on the North American continent. Bibb urged enslaved African Americans to run away and appealed to free Blacks to settle in Canada and take up farming in order to be self-sufficient. In addition, the delegates praised Canada for giving refuge to Black people:

> Resolved, that we feel truly grateful, as a people, to her Britannic Majesty's just and powerful government, for the protection afforded us; and are fully persuaded from the known fertility of the soil, and salubrity of climate of the milder regions of Canada West, that this is, by far, the most desirable place of resort for colored people, to be found on the American continent.

## THE JOHN ANDERSON TRIAL

The John Anderson extradition trial was an event that galvanized the Black and abolitionist communities in Toronto. Anderson was born enslaved in Missouri. In 1851, he decided to flee to Canada and freedom. A white slaveholder, Seneca Diggs, tried to prevent Anderson's flight. A tussle ensued in which Anderson pulled a knife and stabbed the slaveholder. Diggs later died. However, Anderson made his way to Canada and, aided by abolitionists, he found work. Anderson moved to Brantford, where he was employed as a mason. He even bought a house. In 1859, he confided to a "friend" the story of his escape. This "friend" promptly told the authorities and in no time Anderson was apprehended and arrested.

The government of the United States, on hearing that Anderson had been arrested, called for his immediate return so he could be tried in an American court on the charge of murder.

The Court of the Queen's Bench in Toronto, presided over by Chief Justice John Beverley Robinson, ruled on November 15, 1861, that

Anderson had to be sent back to the United States to face trial. There was a huge outcry at Robinson's ruling. Everyone knew that, if returned, Anderson would face certain death. Missouri was known for its "lynch law." It was a slave state in which Blacks had few or no rights.

The media, especially the Toronto *Globe*, castigated Chief Justice Robinson for his decision. The *Globe* reported that Canada was known as a refuge for freedom seekers, and if Anderson were to be returned, American slave catchers could easily come into Canada and claim their alleged slaves on trumped-up charges. Indeed, it had happened before. Toronto was in an uproar. Blacks met in the churches and denounced the ruling, vowing to ensure that Anderson would not be returned to Missouri. The abolitionist community held meetings at city hall and at St. Lawrence Hall. One noted American abolitionist named Gerrit Smith travelled from upstate New York to speak at St. Lawrence Hall. Smith urged the Black and abolitionist communities to prevent the extradition of Anderson. Even the mayor of Montreal, who was very ill, rose from his sickbed to address a public meeting in support of John Anderson in that city.

John Anderson in Montreal, 1861.

Meanwhile, John Anderson's lawyer and members of the Black and abolitionist communities appealed to the Privy Council in England. This was the highest level to which Canadian lawyers could appeal in the British Empire at that time, and so its decision would be final. The Privy Council ruled in favour of Anderson, noting that slavery was wrong and against "natural rights" and that Anderson was justified in defending himself against a man who wanted to enslave him.

However, even before news of the British decision arrived in Toronto, the Court of Common Pleas, presided over by Judge Henry Draper at

The trial of John Anderson was held in Osgoode Hall in 1861. The building is still standing on the corner of Queen Street and University Avenue.

Toronto's Osgoode Hall, took advantage of a technicality in the Missouri court's petition to rule that Anderson should not be extradited. There was great rejoicing in the city. Marches, dinners, and meetings were held by Black Torontonians celebrating Anderson's victory. Anderson himself gave speeches and thanked his Black and white supporters. A few months later, still fearing for his safety (he thought the Americans would still try to extradite him) Anderson travelled first to Montreal and then to England, where he attended college. He later migrated to Liberia, West Africa.

Toronto's Black women and men drew on their own resources to build a viable political life in the city. African Canadians sometimes made alliances with sympathetic whites in their struggle for a life of dignity. The Anti-Slavery Society of Canada is a sterling example of Black and white co-operation in the fight against racism, slavery, and discrimination.

The various reform organizations, such as the Provincial Union, the Queen Victoria Benevolent Society, and the Ladies Freedman's Aid Society, should be seen not only as philanthropic groups, but, given the nature of their activism, also as political organizations. Years later, a son of African Virginian immigrants to the city would rise to the top of Toronto's politics. William Hubbard, a baker by trade, was elected to what today would be called city council in 1894 and served as acting deputy mayor of Toronto intermittently between 1904 and 1907.

Dr. Anderson Ruffin Abbott in Civil War uniform.

# nine

# BLACK TORONTONIANS IN THE CIVIL WAR

MANY AFRICAN CANADIANS fought in the Union Army during the American Civil War. The conflict arose over the issue of "state's rights," specifically the right of each territory or state to choose between being a slave state or a free state. The election of President Abraham Lincoln, who opposed expansion of slavery into new territories and took office on March 4, 1861, brought matters to a head. When the slave states of the American South began to separate from the Union over this issue, the Civil War broke out in April 1861.

Toronto has always had close ties to the United States. As an important port on the Great Lakes, the commercial enterprises of the city regularly did business with American cities like Buffalo and Rochester. Railways linked Toronto with Chicago and Detroit, and with upper New York State. Companies that did business in both countries maintained offices in both Toronto and U.S. cities.

Canadian newspapers such as the *Globe* regularly reported on American events. Toronto was also a hotbed of antislavery activism, involving both Black and white abolitionists, for decades before the Civil War. Indeed, the city played a pivotal role between British and American antislavery interests. Abolitionists in Canada worked with both U.S. and British antislavery forces toward bringing an end to the institution of slavery in the American South.

American-born Black people who migrated to Toronto remained committed to abolishing slavery in the United States, as well as to helping make conditions better for Black Americans living in the Northern states. They often maintained ties with family, friends, and associates south of the border. Many who fled Southern slavery left behind parents, dearly loved husbands or wives, and even children, as Deborah and Perry Brown had been forced to do. Free African Americans who had moved from cities like Philadelphia, New York, and Cincinnati in search of better opportunities for their families stayed in touch with relatives and business partners in the United States.

Foremost in everyone's mind in the 1850s was the threat of war within the United States. The North and South could not agree whether slavery should be allowed in the newly forming states of the western frontier. As the conflict continued, and after war was formally declared, it became apparent that if the Union Army of the North defeated the Confederate Army of the South, slavery in the United States would end.

Black Canadians made a very significant contribution to the war effort, and so helped free more than four million enslaved African Americans. Many families living in Toronto sent their sons to fight and die so that the institution of slavery would forever be destroyed in North America.

On January 1, 1863, President Abraham Lincoln issued the Emancipation Proclamation, which promised freedom for those enslaved in the states of the Confederacy. But it did not mention states that had remained in the Union — such as Kentucky and Maryland, even though slavery was legal and common in both. Toronto's African Canadian churches held services for men going to fight on the Union side in the Civil War. After two years of bloody fighting, President Lincoln had finally decided to enlist the thousands of African Americans who volunteered for the Union Army. African Canadians also flocked to enlist in Michigan's 102nd Colored Troops, the 5th Massachusetts (Colored) Cavalry, the 5th Massachusetts (Colored) Infantry, and other units, while yet others joined the American Navy, as well. Mary Ann Shadd Cary, an important abolitionist and newspaper publisher who once lived in Toronto, moved from Chatham, Canada West, to Detroit to become a rare female recruiting officer for the Union Army. Harriet Tubman also recruited Black men for the Union Army.

Canadian Black men who went to fight ranged from sailors and waiters through physicians and teachers. Not all came home. Abraham Brown died in South Carolina in 1863, only six months after he joined up, but Privates William Jackson and John E. Annick, of Toronto, both survived the hostilities and were discharged at the end of the war in August of 1865.

Medical men from Toronto rose high in the ranks of Black Union Army officers. Dr. Alexander T. Augusta, from Virginia, had trained at Toronto's Trinity College before becoming the official physician for the House of Industry, as the city's "poor house" was called. A distinguished surgeon, he was the first Black major commissioned in the Union Army and for a time directed the Freedmen's Bureau Hospital at Washington, D.C., before entering other theatres of the war. After the conflict was over, Dr. Augusta stayed in the U.S., serving as the director of the Freedmen's Bureau Hospital in Savannah, Georgia. In 1868 he became the first Black faculty member of an American medical school when he received his appointment at Washington's Howard University.

Dr. A.T. (Alexander Thomas) Augusta in his Civil War uniform.

Wilson Ruffin Abbott and Ellen Toyer Abbott's brilliant son, Anderson Ruffin Abbott, was the first Canadian-born Black doctor to graduate as an M.D. After completing his formal studies at the Toronto School of Medicine, he learned to practise as a physician under Dr. A.T. Augusta in Toronto. Also a distinguished surgeon serving under contract to the Union Army, Dr. Abbott became assistant director and surgeon-in-chief of what would become the Freedmen's Hospital in Washington, D.C. He was entertained at the White House and later received from Mrs. Lincoln a shawl once worn by the president, as a token of esteem. He went on to be the first Black coroner for Kent County in Ontario, practised in Dundas, and then returned to the U.S. as the director of Chicago's Provident Hospital. He retired to Toronto, joining the York Pioneers Historical Society and devoting the rest of his life to intellectual pursuits.

In April of 1865, the Civil War ended. The forces that fought to keep the North and the South together as one united country had prevailed. The threat of separation of the Southern states was over. There was much celebration in the African American and African Canadian community. Then a terrible thing happened. President Lincoln was shot in Ford's Theatre on April 14 and died the next morning. Toronto was plunged into mourning. Both Black and white churches held memorial services, and a mass meeting of Black Torontonians assembled to commemorate the life and good deeds of the man they credited with abolishing slavery.

Tintype of an unidentified Black soldier in the Union Army during the Civil War (1861–65).

With the end of the Civil War and the emancipation of enslaved African Americans, the engines of the Underground Railroad grew silent. Black people were finally free to make their own way — to live off the sweat of their own brows. Some

African Canadians felt the need to make a "return trip" south to find and reunite with families and loved ones from whom they had been separated. Many well-educated Black Canadians became teachers, doctors, lawyers, and politicians in the United States during America's Reconstruction Era, which was intended to rebuild society after the war and help the formerly enslaved make their way in freedom. It is a common belief amongst historians that most African Canadians returned to the United States following the Civil War. New research, however, shows that many people remained in Canada and brought their now-free relatives back to live with them in their new country, as Deborah and Perry Brown did with their daughter and granddaughter.

Black soldiers in the Civil War, Company E, 4th U.S. Infantry, Fort Lincoln, Virginia.

Unfortunately, the tide of history shifted again as Europe colonized Africa, beginning in the 1880s. The rise of Jim Crow laws[1] in the United States barred African Americans from enjoying the fruits of full citizenship. Reconstruction was swept away and, in its wake, a new form of racist society emerged. Black people in Canada did not have many racist laws enacted against them, but nevertheless they were greatly affected by this climate of anti-Black feeling. Canada's role as a haven for freedom seekers was no more. White Canadians were no longer as accepting of Blacks as they had appeared to be before the Civil War. Caricatures of Black people appeared routinely in the press and mass media. In 1850, no fewer than sixteen Black businesses had thrived in the elegant King Street shopping district. By the turn of the century, Black businesses were few and far between. African Canadians were kept at the bottom of the social class system, often in the lowest-paying and most servile occupations. It was a cruel twist of fate for those who had risked everything to live under "the Lion's paw of British freedom," as it was termed. But African Canadians forged on, believing a better day would dawn.

Thomas Powers Casey owned a successful barber and hairdressing shop in St. Catharines before relocating to the Rossin House Hotel, Toronto, in 1867. Here, Thomas Powers Casey is shown with two of his three daughters. From left to right: Henrietta Margaret (who married Philip Judah) and Hannah Elizabeth (who married Levi Lightfoot).

(inset) Daughter Mary Ann Casey became the wife of Dr. Anderson Ruffin Abbott. Photo circa 1875.

# ten

# NOTABLE BLACK TORONTONIANS

THE BLACK FREEDOM seekers and free persons who made Toronto their home during the Underground Railroad era contributed greatly to the growth and development of the city. Our research unveiled the biographies — some quite extensive — of many of these people. All of the personages encountered, whether they led public or obscure lives, left a mark on history. The biographies that follow represent a broad cross-section of remarkable individuals who contributed both to the development of early Toronto's vibrant Black culture and to the growth and maturation of the city as a whole.

## THE ABBOTT FAMILY

Wilson Ruffin Abbott, born of a free woman in Richmond, Virginia, would become the wealthiest African Canadian resident of Toronto. He arrived in his new home in 1835 with his wife, Ellen Toyer Abbott, a free Black woman from

Baltimore who taught her husband to read and write. Having met on a Mississippi steamboat, they had left behind in Mobile, Alabama, a prosperous grocery business that had aroused envy and resentment on the part of their white competitors. Threatened with arson, the Abbotts left — life was too repressive and dangerous in the American South for free Black families. They moved first to New York and then to Upper Canada.

Abbott was a lifelong opponent of slavery and racial oppression, serving on numerous committees and as part of various organizations throughout his long life. He bought the freedom of his wife's sister, Jane Toyer, and helped establish self-help and benevolent groups, as well as being a founder of the Coloured Wesleyan Methodist Church and the Anti-Slavery Society of Canada. His wife, Ellen Toyer Abbott, was president of the Queen Victoria Benevolent Society, a Black women's charitable organization with branches across the province. In his later life, Abbott ran for the Toronto city council, although the Toronto *Colonist* of January 18, 1848, shows that he was defeated by Robert Britton Denison.

Abbott's name appeared frequently in the city newspapers, both as an advocate for urban improvements and as a spokesperson and political pundit rallying support for Reform politicians, including George Brown, publisher of the Toronto *Globe* and a future Father of Confederation. When Wilson Ruffin Abbott passed away in 1876, he left a substantial estate including more than forty houses from Owen Sound on Georgian Bay, to Toronto and Hamilton.

The Abbotts had four sons and five daughters but only three lived to adulthood. All were educated and accomplished individuals, and the second son, Anderson, was the first Canadian-born Black doctor. He became one of only eight Black surgeons in the Union Army and was assistant director of the Freedmen's Hospital in Washington, D.C. Another son, William Henson Abbott, graduated from Victoria College and was ordained as a British Methodist Episcopal minister. He pastored a congregation in Hamilton for a time and later served as an African Methodist Episcopal minister in Atlantic City, New Jersey, and then Boston. Wilson and Ellen Abbott's daughter Amelia Etta, born in 1842, was noted for her appreciation for the arts. She married John Watkins, a Toronto law clerk. Their daughter Helene Amelia, a great favourite with her uncle Anderson Ruffin Abbott, married Bruce Yancy of Edina, Minnesota. He was from a locally prominent Black family whose members were known for their musical talent.

## ADOLPHUS AND PHILIP JUDAH

The Judahs were another important African American immigrant family to make their mark on Toronto life. Adolphus was born in Richmond, Virginia, and came to Toronto in 1848. He married Ellen Toyer Abbott's sister, Jane, and rapidly rose to prominence through his dedication to the causes of education and self-sufficiency for the African Canadian community. He vigorously encouraged Black Torontonians to participate in the political life of the city. Judah was a staunch supporter of antislavery activities in Toronto and was central to the establishment of the Coloured Regular Baptist congregation on Terauley (Bay) Street. He was a founder of the Provincial Union Association, the organizational arm of the *Provincial Freeman* newspaper, and of the Association for the Education and Elevation of Coloured People.

Adolphus H. Judah later moved to Chatham, Canada West, where he supported the Elgin Association and the organized colony of formerly enslaved and free Blacks founded by Reverend William

Philip Judah and his wife Henrietta (Casey) on the porch of the home of William P. Hubbard, 660 Broadview, following the death of his first wife, Caroline, in 1915.

King at Buxton. His son, Philip, who had won prizes in 1859 while a young student at Louisa Street School, continued to play an important role in Black Toronto's political and community life. He married Caroline Weaver of Chatham. They operated a fancy green grocery in Toronto's St. Patrick's Ward, at the northwest corner of Queen Street at Beverley. The building is still standing today. Their beautiful house was on Broadview Avenue, overlooking the valley of the Don River. After Caroline Judah passed away, Philip took as his bride Henrietta Margaret Casey. She had been living next door with her sister Mary Ann Casey, the wife of Dr. Anderson Ruffin Abbott.

A directory listing for Hickman, W. and Hickman, Wm., Jr. From *Rowsell's City of Toronto and County of York Directory, for 1850–51.*

## THE HICKMAN FAMILY

The Hickmans came to Toronto in the 1830s from Virginia. William Hickman Sr., a barber, had been freed because he fought in both the American Revolution and in the War of 1812 on the American side. But new legislation passed after the Nat Turner Rebellion of 1831 meant that formerly enslaved Virginians could not stay in the state even after they received their freedom. He and his wife Elizabeth (known as Betsey) moved to Toronto with their son and daughter, along with other members of their extended family, including Philip Gallego and his wife, Charlotte, who was Mrs. Hickman's sister. Arriving in about 1833, they came with money to purchase land on York Street, south of Osgoode Hall, and to start a barbering business. It was first located at the St. Lawrence Market, and in later years on York.

Hickman took an active part in the city's early antislavery activities. Along with J.C. Brown and Stephen Dutton, two of the founders of the

Wilberforce Settlement located north of London, the Hickmans also owned land in the Oro area north of Barrie, where a number of Black veterans of the War of 1812 had been awarded land grants.

Betsey and William Hickman's son and grandson, both named William, were business people in Toronto by the 1850s. They owned land on York Street, just south of Osgoode Hall, and operated a barber shop a..d grocery stores in the area. Nearby were a number of other Black-owned businesses. Just across the street, for example, was the fancy ladies' accessory shop of Mrs. M.O. Augusta. Next door to the Hickman home was a house owned by Betsey's nephew, Peter Gallego, a very promising Black student at the university. The Hickman family had a practical approach to helping fugitive slaves: they built extra housing in the backyards of their downtown properties so that newcomers would have somewhere to live when they first came to the city. In the Toronto street directories, these were listed as "rear premises," and housed a long series of incoming freedom seekers who paid only nominal rents.

## JAMES MINK

Mr. Mink was a familiar sight on Toronto's downtown streets, for he operated the city's largest livery stable and several stagecoach lines, as well as a fancy hotel, the Mansion House. He was first located near the corner of Richmond and York Streets and then moved to 21 Adelaide Street East, at the head of Toronto Street. The livery stable finally ended up at Queen and Terauley (Bay) Streets. Mink was the son of an enslaved couple brought to Canada with a United Empire Loyalist family, the Herkimers, who settled at the east end of Lake Ontario. James's brother George Mink operated a stagecoach business and hotel in Kingston and, between the two of them, the Minks dominated postal transport connecting Kingston and Toronto, as well as the transfer of prisoners between Kingston Penitentiary and the Toronto jail. James Mink often billed the mayor and city council for the use of his carriages and horses.

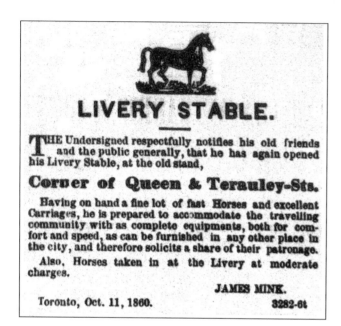

**LIVERY STABLE.**

THE Undersigned respectfully notifies his old friends and the public generally, that he has again opened his Livery Stable, at the old stand,

**Corner of Queen & Terauley-Sts.**

Having on hand a fine lot of fast Horses and excellent Carriages, he is prepared to accommodate the travelling community with as complete equipments, both for comfort and speed, as can be furnished in any other place in the city, and therefore solicits a share of their patronage.

Also, Horses taken in at the Livery at moderate charges.

JAMES MINK.

Toronto, Oct. 11, 1860. 3282-6t

An advertisement in the *Globe*, October 17, 1860, for James Mink's livery stable at its final location at Queen and Terauley Streets.

There is a persistent myth that in his later life James Mink spent much of his fortune rescuing his daughter. She had supposedly married a (white) Yorkshire cabman who subsequently sold her into slavery in the American South. Genealogist Guylaine Pétrin has proven that this story was invented by a Scottish novelist who published his article in *Blackwoods Magazine* in 1860. It has been endlessly reprinted ever since. The tale, which even appeared in Toronto newspapers in later years, is utterly without foundation. In fact, Mary Mink married a well-respected Black man named William Johnson. They lived in Toronto and then moved to Niagara Falls, New York, where he worked at the Cataract House hotel, and later to Milwaukee, Wisconsin. There she died in the arms of her family in 1878. The Mary (or Minnie) Mink story is, however, exactly the sort of falsehood invented by racist nineteenth-century white authors when confronted with the manifest success of a very astute, well-to-do, and propertied African Canadian gentleman.

An article in the New York *Tribune* of October 24, 1856, described James Mink as follows: "The livery stable keeper is a fine example, physically of the pure black man; in countenance good-humored, open, and sensible, stout in figure and inclined to obesity, in manner equally free from rudeness and servility." The Toronto *Mail* of July 2, 1880, also gave a complimentary description of Mr. Mink, while providing an impassioned rebuttal to the myth of "Minnie Mink" that had just been republished, with embellishments, by the Chicago *Times*. The *Mail* article closed with the following tribute: "The Chicago story is therefore a huge myth and a gross libel on the Mink family. Miss Mink received an excellent education, and was most accomplished, and her father was a man respected by every Torontonian." According to Pétrin, "James Mink was buried in the Toronto Necropolis cemetery and, unusually for one of the city's Black citizens, his death at the age of 70 years and 10 months was announced in the *Globe* newspaper of Monday, 14 September 1868."

## THORNTON AND LUCIE BLACKBURN

Thornton and Lucie Blackburn were freedom seekers from Kentucky who started Toronto's first taxi business. Their 1831 escape to liberty made history in both Canada and the United States. The Blackburns' remarkable story came to light as the result of a 1985 archaeological excavation conducted by Dr. Karolyn Frost Smardz, one of the co-authors of this book. It was the first Underground Railroad site ever dug in Canada.

Thornton and Lucie fled enslavement in Louisville in a daring daylight escape by steamboat on the Independence Day weekend of 1831, armed with forged freedom papers. They first made their way to Detroit, where they were captured two years later. The Blackburns were rescued in a highly dramatic series of events. Lucie was spirited out of the Detroit jail in disguise. The next day Thornton was freed by a crowd of more than two hundred people, and both he and his wife crossed the Detroit River to Canada. This became known ever after as the "Blackburn Riots of 1833." The couple were briefly jailed in Sandwich (now part of Windsor) while the Michigan government demanded their return. They were freed by order of Lieutenant Governor Sir John Colborne and his Executive Council. Their landmark extradition case resulted in the creation of Canada's first refugee reception policy and set the tone for fugitive slave cases until the Civil War.

Arriving in Toronto in 1834, the Blackburns built a small frame house on what is now Eastern Avenue at Sackville Street. Thornton's first job was as a waiter at Osgoode Hall. Soon, though, he and his wife went into business for themselves. They ordered a carriage built, painted it red and yellow, named their cab "The City,"

CHAPTER CCI.

## THE FIRST CAB IN THE CITY.

The Early History of Public Conveyances and Some of the Men Who Drove Them.

East of Parliament street is a section of the city abounding in short, narrow streets, thickly built up with houses of moderate size. Eastern avenue is one of the thoroughfares traversing this district. No. 54 of this street is a very small one storey frame building, painted almost black by wind and weather. Here for more than fifty years has lived a well known coloured man named Thornton Blackburn. In one of the doors in his house he points out to the visitor a panel shattered by a bullet during the Mackenzie rebellion. Mr. Blackburn came from the United States to Toronto, accompanied by his wife, who is still living, in 1884. For several years he found employment as a table waiter at Osgoode Hall. Previous to this cabs had made their first appearance in Montreal copied from a vehicle then popular in London. Mr. Blackburn obtained the pattern of a Montreal cab and taking it to Paul Bishop, a French Canadian, whose name of L'Eveque —the Bishop—had been Anglicized in Upper Canada, he ordered one made from the design furnished. Bishop, who was a mechanic of great skill, and counted as the best lockmaker in Canada, had a shop at the north-east corner of Sherbourne and Duke streets. He accepted Mr. Blackburn's commission, and in 1837 he delivered to him the first cab built in Upper Canada. This cab has been on exhibition at the York Pioneer's log house in the Exhibition grounds. It was named " The City." The cab was painted yellow and red. The entrance for passengers was from the rear. There was accommodation in it for four passengers. The driver sat on his box in front. One horse drew the vehicle. For several years Mr. Blackburn had the monopoly of the cab business in Toronto. It was found to be so profitable a pursuit that others were tempted to engage in it. One Monday morning Owen, Miller & Mills, carriage makers, on the south side of King street, a little west of York street, turned out for Guest & Griffin, the proprietors of a livery stable on King street east, about the site of Hugh Miller's drug store, six cabs. These were like a little dark-coloured sentry box mounted on wheels.

Toronto *Telegram* article about the Blackburns and their taxi business.

and operated their highly successful taxi business for more than three decades. Thornton and Lucie became prosperous members of Toronto's Black community. The couple participated in antislavery and community-building activities, and Thornton was a delegate to the 1851 Convention of Coloured People at St. Lawrence Hall. Lucie gave some of the first monies to build Little Trinity Church, and the couple generously donated both time and money to helping other freedom seekers settle in their adopted home.

Lifelong friends with Ann Maria Jackson and her children, it was likely the Blackburns with whom the Jackson family stayed when they first arrived in Toronto. Children's toys from the mid-nineteenth century were discovered under the floorboards during the 1985 dig. The Blackburns themselves were childless.

The Blackburn site excavations offered insight into the lives and experiences of freedom seekers in early Toronto. Artifacts included household china and glassware, cutlery, and construction nails from their modest house and the storey-and-a-half barn where they stored their taxi and stabled the horse that pulled it. From the kitchen fireplace excavators recovered bones from fish, rabbits, and ducks that the Blackburns caught in the nearby marshes at the foot of the Don River. More than three thousand schoolchildren took part in the dig, which received more publicity than any site in Canadian history after Louisbourg.

In 1999, the Canadian government designated the Blackburns "Persons of National Historic Significance" for their important contribution to the growth of Toronto. Over one April weekend in 2002, twin plaques in their honour were erected in Louisville, Kentucky, and Toronto, Canada. This was the first commemoration of an Underground Railroad journey ever carried out between the United States and Canada. Today there is a beautiful steel-cut sculpture at the Inglenook Community School grounds representing the twelve thousand years of human activity at the site where the Blackburn home was once located, and George Brown College named a new venue, opened in 2015, "The Lucie and Thornton Blackburn Convention Centre."

## REVEREND W.M. MITCHELL

Most African Canadians did not leave a record of their thoughts and feelings about life during the era of the Underground Railroad. One of the exceptions was Reverend William M. Mitchell, a Baptist minister and abolitionist who is perhaps best known for writing *The Under-Ground Railroad* (1860).

Mitchell was born free in Guildford County, North Carolina, to a Native American mother and African American father in about 1836. His parents died when he was quite young, and he was raised by local authorities. Mitchell was apprenticed to a planter for twelve years and managed a plantation for the last five years of his indenture. He witnessed all the cruelties and abuses of the slave system.

A steel engraving of Reverend William M. Mitchell of Toronto.

As a result of his experiences, after his period of indenture was up, he studied Christianity and devoted himself to the cause of the enslaved. In 1843, Mitchell moved to Ross County, Ohio, with his wife and assisted refugees from bondage on the Underground Railroad. Among those they helped was the famous Eliza Harris, immortalized in Harriet Beecher Stowe's novel *Uncle Tom's Cabin*. She escaped across the Ohio River by jumping from ice floe to ice floe, her child in her arms, so that her infant son — who had already been sold — could not be delivered to the person who bought him.

In 1855, Mitchell became a missionary for the American Baptist Free Mission Society and moved to Ward 3, York Township West. He pastored at the Coloured Regular Baptist Church on Terauley (Bay) and Edward Streets in downtown Toronto and became involved in helping to improve educational opportunities for the Black community in Canada. For example, with Adolphus Judah, he was a member of the "Association for the Education and Elevation of the Coloured People of Canada," a race-uplift organization focused on African Canadian youth. According to 1861 census records, Reverend Mitchell lived with his wife, Eliza, and five children, James, John, Fred J., Eliza E., and Augusta L., who ranged in age from two to sixteen years. Their home was in the semirural area north of the city limits at Bloor Street near Bathurst and they were neighbours of Deborah and Perry Brown. Between 1859 and 1861, Mitchell travelled to England, Ireland, and Scotland on a fundraising tour for his church. It was there that he published his antislavery narrative. Mitchell's was the only volume published before the Civil War that named the highly illegal Underground Railroad in its title. His son James Washington Mitchell was also a Baptist minister in Toronto, from 1874 to 1879, before moving to the U.S.

Transfer-printed soup plate with the illustration *Eliza Crosses the Ohio on the Floating Ice* in *Uncle Tom's Cabin*. Such images reflect the popularity of Harriet Beecher Stowe's famed antislavery novel. Found at the Courthouse Site in St. John's Ward.

## REVEREND WASHINGTON CHRISTIAN

Ordained at New York's Abyssinia Baptist Church in 1822, Reverend Washington Christian organized the first Baptist congregations in Toronto. Aptly named First Baptist Church, his budding congregation of fifteen freedom seekers began meeting in 1826 on the shore of Lake Ontario. After worshipping in a variety of locations including the St. George's Masonic Lodge and a small frame chapel on Lombard Street, Reverend Washington soon shepherded his congregation to its first real church building. It stood at the northeast corner of Queen and Victoria Streets, where St. Michael's Hospital is now. In 1842, Christian went on a fundraising tour to the West Indies to raise money for his church and was so successful that he paid off the mortgage. Attracting to its congregation some of the leading Black families in Toronto, the "First Colored Calvinistic Baptist Church" soon emerged as a centre of Black activism in the city.

Universally known and loved as "Elder Washington," Christian gained a reputation as a "church founder." He travelled frequently in the Niagara Peninsula and the southwestern part of the province and was made a life member of the Amherstburg Baptist Association that linked churches across Canada West with those in Michigan. In his day he was noted for establishing more Baptist churches than any other preacher in Canada, including ones in Toronto, Hamilton, Niagara, and St. Catharines. He died in 1850 after a long life devoted to faith and good works, and lies beside his wife, Ann, in the Toronto Necropolis cemetery.

## RICHARD B. RICHARDS

Richard Butler Richards was a successful merchant who established an early ice business in Toronto. He operated it in partnership with Thomas F. Cary, a Toronto businessman and activist who married Mary Ann Shadd. The Richards were from the United States, probably Fredericksburg, Virginia, as that was the birthplace of Richard's wife, Sarah. They likely came to Canada in the 1830s. Richards is listed with his wife and four children in the Gallego census of Black Torontonians in 1841. By 1854, the Richardses operated four icehouses and by 1861, Richards and his wife Sarah owned a farm with their adult children and other family members in York Township, Ward 3, on Davenport Road. Their daughter Susannah married George Washington Carter, a Toronto barber who became a spokesperson for the Black community in the latter part of the nineteenth century.

## ICE! ICE!! ICE!!

THE Undersigned begs to return his best thanks to his Customers for the liberal patronage he has received for the last nine years, and to announce that he has enlarged and added to the number of his Ice Houses, having now four, which are filled with pure and wholesome Springwater Ice, from Yorkville. He is prepared to supply the same to consumers, by contract or otherwise, during the season, commencing from the 1st of June. In consequence of the increased cost of labor and materials, the price will this year be raised in the same proportion. The Ice will be conveyed by waggon, daily, to places within six miles of Toronto. All orders sent to T. F. Cary, 68 King Street West, will be punctually attended to.

**R. B. RICHARDS.**

Toronto. June 1, 1854.

Advertisement of Richard B. Richard's ice business in the *Provincial Freeman*, July 8, 1854.

Their ice business, valued in 1861 at $1,100, was at the farm location on Davenport. It stored and sold a hundred tons of ice for a total value of $600 annually and employed three male "hands" at an average cost per month of $8. These employees chopped huge frozen blocks from the mill ponds at Yorkville as well as from Ashbridges Bay during the winter and kept the ice insulated with sawdust for sale during the summer months. Mr. Richards employed his children and other relatives in his business and on the farm. In the *Globe* of August 27, 1855, he advertised that deliveries could be had by placing orders at the hairdressing establishment of Thomas F. Cary at Front and King Streets.

Reverend Mitchell, a neighbour and acquaintance, described the Richardses' business concerns as follows:

An ice merchant, who furnishes hotels, public houses, and private families, during the summer with ice, has a farm under good cultivation. His son-in-law has on the same farm a two-story frame house, furnished as well inside as it is finished outside.

R.B. Richards was a respected member and trustee of the Coloured Regular Baptist Church on Terauley (Bay) and Edward Streets in St. John's Ward. This was the same church where Reverend Mitchell served and that was attended by Adolphus Judah and his family. Richard B. Richards passed away in 1879 at the age of seventy-nine, buried by his son-in-law in the Carter family grave at the Toronto Necropolis.

# THE CARY BROTHERS

The Cary brothers, George W., Isaac N., John I., and Thomas F., were free-born Blacks from Virginia who came to Toronto in the 1840s, some of them by way of Cincinnati. They opened several barber saloons that catered to all Torontonians, Black and white. In the 1850s, Thomas joined with Richard B. Richards in the ice business. By 1854, Cary and Richards owned four ice houses; Thomas, however, continued to operate the barber shop with his brothers. They advertised in the *Provincial Freeman* to

> all who wish to be operated upon in the line of either hair cutting, shaving, hair curling or shampooing.

The Cary brothers were also strong abolitionists. They campaigned against racial prejudice, led Black self-help organizations, organized Black conventions, and urged the city's African Canadians to abandon the Conservative Party and support the Reform Party (the Liberals). George W. Cary and Isaac N. Cary both spoke at a "Meeting of Colored Electors" held August 23, 1858, in favour of George Brown's candidacy in the coming elections. In 1857, Thomas F. Cary married Mary Ann Shadd, publisher of the *Provincial Freeman*. Thomas died in 1860. Isaac N. Cary married Mary Bibb, widow of Henry Bibb.

Both Isaac N. Cary and his brother George, who had immigrated from Cincinnati to the Dawn Settlement in the southwestern part of the province in 1842, were supporters of the Haitian emigration movement that was active in Canada West during the 1850s. In December of 1859 John J. Cary and George W. Cary were prominent at a Toronto meeting held at First Baptist Church on Queen Street. Its purpose was to raise money for the family of martyred white abolitionist John Brown, who had been hanged for organizing a raid on the military arsenal at Harpers Ferry, Virginia. William Wells Brown, an abolitionist writer, described Isaac N. Cary as "one of the most enterprising and intellectual men in Canada, [who] is deeply interested in the moral, social, and political elevation of all classes."

## MARY ANN SHADD CARY

Mary Ann Shadd Cary was perhaps the best-known female abolitionist in Canada. Born in Wilmington, Delaware, of free Black parents, she was the daughter of Harriet and Abraham Doras Shadd. Her father was a respected abolitionist and leader of the Black convention movement. The family moved to Pennsylvania so that Mary Ann and her siblings could attend a private Quaker school for Black children. After graduating, Mary Ann taught school in various cities in the northeastern United States but, in the fall of 1851, moved to Windsor, Canada West, and opened a school for Black children there.

In Windsor, Mary Ann worked with Henry and Mary Bibb, but because they had a disagreement about the administration of her school and, later, other issues, she decided to establish and publish her views in her own newspaper. After putting out a premiere issue in Windsor, she began publishing her weekly paper in Toronto in March 1854. From its office at 5 King Street East, the *Provincial Freeman* spoke out against slavery and offered information for members of the African Canadian community about issues ranging from education to agriculture, racial uplift, and self-improvement. In 1852, Mary Ann also published a volume entitled *A Plea for Emigration; or, Notes of Canada West*, encouraging African Americans to move to Canada. After a year in Toronto, Shadd moved her paper to Chatham and continued to publish it there into the year 1860.

In 1857, Mary Ann married Thomas F. Cary, a widowed Toronto businessman and partner of Richard B. Richards in his ice business. Thomas brought three children to the marriage, and he and Mary Ann had two children, Sarah and Linton. Even with a family, she continued to tour the province and the northern United States speaking out on behalf of the antislavery cause, Canadian emigration, and other matters dear to her heart. With the death of her husband in 1860 and the

Mary Ann Shadd Cary, educator, community activist, lawyer, and first Black woman publisher/editor of a newspaper in North America. In 1994, Shadd Cary was designated a Person of National Historic Significance in Canada.

The *Provincial Freeman* (1853–60) was based in Toronto from 1854 to 1855 before moving to Chatham, Canada West. The paper provided news by and for the Black community of Canada.

outbreak of the Civil War a year later, Mary Ann had the distinction of being one of a very few Black women recruiting officers for the Union Army. She later became the second Black woman to obtain a law degree in 1883 from Howard University in Washington, D.C. She devoted the rest of her life to the cause of the Black community, women's equality, and the long struggle for Black women's right to vote.

## ANN MARIA JACKSON

Ann Maria Jackson was a freedom seeker who fled from her Delaware slaveholder in the spring of 1858. Going by way of Wilmington and then Philadelphia, Mrs. Jackson made it to St. Catharines and then to Toronto. Jackson's flight was spectacular because she "stole away" not only herself, but also her seven children, aged two to seventeen. This was a rare feat indeed, when one considers that most of those who fled slavery on the Underground Railroad were young men in their prime, young men most likely to be sold away from their families. It was difficult for women to run away secretly, especially with young children.

While in St. Catharines, Jackson was aided by abolitionist Reverend Hiram Wilson, who sent her on to Toronto. Once there, it is believed she and her children

(left) Ann Maria Jackson and her seven children escaped from Delaware, a remarkable feat of courage and determination.

(right) This stamp was issued in 2019 in honour of Albert Jackson, the first postman of African descent in Toronto.

stayed with Lucie and Thornton Blackburn. Members of the Anti-Slavery Society helped her establish herself in the city. Her first home was a house at 8 Terauley (Bay) Street north of Queen, owned by Wilson and Ellen Abbott. Jackson worked as a washerwoman and lived for most of her life in the city on Elizabeth Street in St. John's Ward.

The Jackson story is not just one of triumph. Tragedy is the other thread that holds this narrative together. Just before her flight, Ann Maria's two elder sons had been sold away. Jackson's husband, a free man, went mad as a result and died in the Poor House. It was this loss of two children and her husband, and the prospect of the sale of more of her young ones, that prompted her to gather her family and risk all in the desperate flight to freedom. Happily, both her elder sons later fled to Canada and rejoined their family. Ann Maria Jackson's youngest child was Albert Jackson, who would grow up to be Toronto's first Black postman. A postage stamp was issued in his honour in 2019.

## CECELIA JANE REYNOLDS

Cecelia was only fifteen when she arranged her own flight to freedom in the summer of 1846. Enslaved from birth, she grew up in the Thruston household in Louisville, Kentucky. Cecelia's father Adam was a skilled rope-maker but had been sold away to the slave traders when Cecelia was only six. She herself was given to Fanny Thruston to serve as a lady's maid when she was only nine, but always longed to be free. When she found out the Thrustons were planning to holiday at Niagara Falls, Cecelia saw her chance.

Underground Railroad operators in Kentucky passed word up the rivers and roads all the way to Canada that this young girl would need their help. The Thrustons stayed at the luxurious Cataract House hotel in Niagara Falls, New York. Guests did not know that the hotel workers, all Black, were secretly assisting freedom seekers on their way north. One of them was Moseby Hubbard, whose son William Peyton Hubbard would one day become Toronto's first African Canadian deputy mayor.

While the Thrustons toured the sights, Cecelia was spirited away across the Niagara River. Steamboat waiter Benjamin Pollard Holmes helped her reach Toronto. There she married Benjamin at St. James Cathedral in November 1846, and became the stepmother of two little boys, Ben Alexander Holmes and James Thomas Holmes.

Cecelia missed her family in Kentucky, so she learned how to write and began to correspond with Fanny. Now married with children of her own, Fanny Thruston Ballard's first letter to Cecelia arrived in 1852. It contained shocking news. Fanny and her husband wanted Cecelia and Benjamin to pay $600 to buy Mary Reynold's freedom. It was a huge sum — a house in Toronto's St. John's Ward might sell for $150. So Cecelia and Benjamin crossed the Atlantic to earn the money to purchase Cecelia's mother and set her free. Benjamin travelled on to Australia, where gold had been discovered, while Cecelia found a job in England. But a series of misfortunes sent Cecelia back to Canada alone. In the spring of 1854, she had a little girl she named Mamie, after her mother. Benjamin came back to Toronto a year later but died in 1859.

Cecelia moved to Rochester, New York, where she is believed to have helped Frederick Douglass, the renowned abolitionist, with his Underground Railroad activities and his abolitionist newspaper. Later on, Cecelia remarried. She accompanied her husband William to the battlefields of the Civil War, and then took her family to Kentucky, where she was reunited with her mother, now a free woman. Cecelia kept her Toronto home as a rental property until the 1880s, when she sold it to Francis Griffin Simpson, a community leader and shoemaker who lived next door. In 2015, archaeologists preparing a downtown parking lot for the building of the new Ontario Courthouse brought the remains of Cecelia and Benjamin's Toronto home again to light.

## DR. ALEXANDER T. AND MRS. M.O. AUGUSTA

Mrs. Mary O. Augusta was a busy and pioneering woman. She owned a "fancy dry goods and dressmaking" establishment at Adelaide and York Streets, right in the midst of downtown Toronto. From Mrs. Augusta the women of Toronto bought the latest in fashion "from Paris and London." Her husband, Dr. Alexander T. Augusta, was a distinguished Toronto doctor and surgeon. But achieving that position had been challenging. Born in Virginia to free Black parents, Dr. Augusta had hoped to study medicine at the University of Pennsylvania but was denied admission because he was African American. He then took up private study.

Migrating to Toronto in the early 1850s, Alexander T. Augusta studied medicine at the University of Toronto and graduated in 1860 with a medical degree from Trinity College. He went into private practice, worked at the Toronto Hospital, and was medical supervisor of the "House of Industry," or the Poor House. In addition, Dr. Augusta owned and operated a pharmacy on Yonge Street just north of Dundas. An antislavery activist, A.T. Augusta helped found The

Provincial Association for the Education and Elevation of the Coloured People of Canada. Anderson Ruffin Abbott, son of Wilson and Ellen Toyer Abbott, gained his practical education after he graduated from the Toronto School of Medicine by practising under Dr. Augusta.

The Augustas made significant business, social, and cultural contributions to the city of Toronto. However, in 1863, Dr. Augusta was to be found on the battlefields of the American Civil War. He became the U.S. Army's first Black doctor and held the rank of major. After the war, Augusta remained in the U.S. In Washington, he helped establish the Freedmen's Hospital, directed the Freedmen's Hospital at Savannah, Georgia, and then returned to Washington to become the first African American member of a medical faculty when he taught at Howard University. Dr. Augusta lies in Arlington National Cemetery, among the honoured Union veterans of the American Civil War.

**NEW DRUG STORE.**

**CENTRAL MEDICAL HALL.**

**A. T. AUGUSTA**

BEGS to announce to his Friends and the Public generally, that he has OPENED the Store on Yonge Street, one door south of Elm Street, with a New and Choice Selection of

DRUGS, MEDICINES,

*Patent Medicines, Perfumery,*

DYE-STUFFS, &c.,

and trusts, by strict attention to his business, to merit a share of their patronage.

*Physicians' Prescriptions, accurately prepared.*

LEECHES APPLIED.

Cupping, Bleeding, and Teeth extracted.

The Proprietor, or a competent Assistant, always in attendance.

Toronto, March 30, 1855.        6-1y

The apothecary shop owned and operated by Dr. A.T. Augusta was advertised in the *Provincial Freeman*, October 13, 1855.

## THOMAS SMALLWOOD

Thomas Smallwood was born enslaved in Maryland in 1801 and obtained his freedom, along with that of his sister, at the age of thirty years. He was a deeply religious man, employed at the Washington Naval Yards. Disillusioned with the aims of the American Colonization Society that sought to remove free Blacks from the United States and send them to the West African colony of Liberia, he began working with abolitionists to help freedom seekers on their way out of slavery. Smallwood helped to lay the groundwork for a network of Underground Railroad routes through Washington, D.C., that would endure from the early 1840s through the time of the American Civil War.

Fearing he was betrayed, Smallwood hurriedly left for Canada West, arriving in Toronto on July 4, 1843. He returned for his family in October, only

A

NARRATIVE

OF

THOMAS SMALLWOOD,

(Coloured Man:)

GIVING AN ACCOUNT

OF HIS

BIRTH—THE PERIOD HE WAS HELD IN SLAVERY—HIS
RELEASE—AND REMOVAL TO CANADA, ETC.

TOGETHER WITH

AN ACCOUNT OF THE UNDERGROUND RAILROAD.

WRITTEN BY HIMSELF.

Toronto:

PRINTED FOR THE AUTHOR BY JAMES STEPHENS, 5, CITY
BUILDINGS, KING STREET EAST.

1851.

Title page of Thomas Smallwood's book.

extricating them and himself from possible arrest with some difficulty. The family lived on York Street near the Hickmans and Gallegos, south of St. John's Ward, where Smallwood operated a saw-making business.

Thomas Smallwood continued his abolitionist efforts once he reached Canada, on at least one occasion travelling as far as Cincinnati to assist in an unsuccessful attempt to rescue a freedom seeker's family. By March 5, 1847, an article in the Toronto *Banner* regarding the formation of the new Black-led British-American Anti-Slavery Society listed Thomas Smallwood as the society president. Other members included Adolphus Judah and Reverend Washington Christian of First Baptist Church.

Much about Smallwood's interesting personality is known because he published his autobiography, *A Narrative of Thomas Smallwood, Colored Man*, in 1851. It detailed his life as an enslaved man, his work as an Underground Railroad conductor, and his experiences in Toronto and the rest of what today is Ontario. He was a leader in the Black and abolitionist communities of Toronto.

Thomas Smallwood was one of the key organizers of the Convention of Coloured People held at Drummondville (now part of Niagara Falls) in August 1847. He was active for many years in the Black convention movement and was a delegate at the 1851 North American Convention of Coloured People in Toronto where he served as one of its vice-presidents. Smallwood helped organize the Emancipation Day events in the city, was a shareholder in the *Provincial Freeman* newspaper, and in 1854 was one of the founders of the Provincial Union Association that raised funds for the *Provincial Freeman*. The organization was intended to "promote literature, general intelligence, active benevolence, and the principles of universal freedom."

# FRANCIS GRIFFIN SIMPSON

One of the more interesting characters to make Toronto his home was a free African American born in 1823 near Schenectady, New York. Francis Griffin Simpson arrived in the city in 1854 and apprenticed as a shoemaker. He took a position with the Anti-Slavery Society of Canada at their King Street office, where he helped arrange employment for incoming freedom seekers.

Simpson soon emerged as a community activist and spokesperson, engaging in a variety of events and organizations and providing leadership to such groups as the Young Men's Excelsior Literary and Debating Society and the "Moral and Mental Improvement Society (African)." He also served on a variety of committees promoting Reform politics. A well-educated man, he often acted as secretary for meetings of Black Torontonians. The Toronto *Globe* of August 24, 1858, published an article entitled "Meeting of Coloured Electors: Unanimity for Mr. Brown," where F.G. Simpson spoke out on behalf of the election of Reform politician George Brown. He was in good company, for others promoting Brown's candidacy included abolitionist brothers Isaac and George Cary. In other meetings and public events, he served alongside James Mink, Wilson Ruffin Abbott, Anderson Ruffin Abbott, Dr. Alexander T. Augusta, Thomas Smallwood, and other community leaders.

In 1862, Mary Ann Shadd Cary's sister Emeline became the bride of Francis's brother, Reverend Henry Simpson. Just a year later, President Lincoln sent three commissioners to Canada West to interview formerly enslaved and free Black residents, as well as school principals, politicians, ministers, and others who were familiar with their circumstances. The chief commissioner, Samuel Gridley Howe, published the results of their inquiries. These were intended to assist the American government in planning for the ultimate freedom of some four million African Americans. Francis Griffin Simpson gave a most informative interview, commenting that prejudice was a constant impediment to the progress of Toronto's Black residents, but that the law and courts did provide some protection. Howe quoted Simpson: "We have shoemakers, carpenters, blacksmiths and tobacco manufacturers. There are three benevolent societies among the colored people — one male society, and two female societies. Then there is one literary and social society. There are

(top) Leather shoe uncovered in the yard of shoemaker and community spokesperson Francis Griffin Simpson, 31 Centre Street. Found at the Courthouse Site in St. John's Ward.

(bottom) Leather sole of the shoe shown above.

men here who have been here between thirty and forty years."

Francis and Elizabeth Simpson had a shop on King Street and lived in St. John's Ward, for a time on Elizabeth Street, and then they moved to Centre Street. They made their home behind Osgoode Hall in a house Francis had built next door to one owned by Cecelia Jane Reynolds. When she was elderly and living in Louisville, he also purchased her house. Archaeological excavations conducted for the building of Ontario's new courthouse in 2015 turned up a wealth of shoemaking equipment and leather scraps from the two adjoining backyards.

In 1882, when Albert Jackson was not allowed to take up his position as a letter carrier because he was African Canadian, the Black community erupted in outrage. Francis Griffin Simpson chaired a committee to protest the injustice. Ultimately, after the intervention of Sir John A. Macdonald, who needed Black voters to support him in the upcoming election, Jackson was finally permitted to deliver mail, a service he proudly provided for more than three decades.

On March 19, 1900, the Toronto *Globe* published this interesting obituary:

### An Old Resident Dead

Mr. Francis Griffin Simpson, aged 68 years, died at the residence of his son, 155 Richmond Street West, on Saturday morning. Mr. Simpson was taken suddenly ill about a week ago with a severe cold, which developed into pneumonia. He was originally from Schenectady, N.Y. but had been a resident of this city for over 45 years. He was a member of the York Pioneers and took a prominent part in the antislavery movement.

In politics, Mr. Simpson was a lifelong Liberal. He is survived by a wife and one son, Mr. Frank Simpson of the Rossin House. The funeral will take place this afternoon at 2:30 o'clock to Mount Pleasant Cemetery.

## APPENDIX

Perhaps the best description of what life was like for Black immigrants comes from a report from the *New York Tribune* reprinted in the April 1, 1858, edition of the *Anti-Slavery Reporter* and entitled "The Negroes of Toronto":

The large and thriving city of Toronto contains a more numerous colored population than any other town of Canada. Out of its 50,000 inhabitants, from 1200 to 1600 are estimated to be colored. Though the great majority belong to the class of unskilled labourers, among them are to be found followers of a great number and variety of occupations. One of them, a man of wealth, lives upon his means … one is a regularly educated physician; three are studying law; one medicine; two at least are master builders, taking contracts, and employing a number of journey men, both white and black; four are grocers, and the store of one of them — the only one we visited was in a good part of the town, handsome, near well stocked and evidently doing a thriving business, the customers being mostly whites; one keeps a large livery-stable, one of the best in town, and is employed to take the mails to and from the post office to the railroad depots, steamboats &c.; several within the precincts of the city are occupied in farming and gardening; others are bricklayers, carpenters, shoemakers, plasterers, blacksmiths, and carters. Many find employment in sawing and chopping the wood, which is the general fuel and the barbers and waiters in hotels and private families are almost exclusively colored men … many of them have accumulated considerable property (especially) among the older residents [in] real estate.

H. Burt Williams' omnibus that operated between the Red Lion Hotel north of Yonge and Bloor Streets and the St. Lawrence Market on Front Street from 1849–62. Owen Staples, artist, ca. 1914.

# eleven

# HOW DO WE KNOW? HISTORY

ONE OF THE QUESTIONS people often ask about history is, "How do you know so much about things that happened such a long time ago?" Finding out about life in nineteenth-century African Canadian Toronto is difficult because many of the people of the time, both Black and white, could not read or, more importantly, write. So there is no personal account of their experiences, recorded in what historians call "their own voice." Also, historians have only recently become interested in the everyday lives of the ordinary people who often worked, raised families, and died without ever doing anything to get their names in the newspaper.

There are very few books written about early Black life in Ontario, and none on Toronto. In fact, this is the very first! Some books about Toronto do mention that Black people, many of whom were once enslaved in the United States, used to live there. But that's about it. So we have to delve deeper to discover the African Canadian story. Fortunately, with the significant number of Black people living in the city by 1860, some records just have to exist.

The first place we look for information are the censuses, which are the government's attempts to count every single person living in Canada in a given year. These are done more or less every ten years. Although the 1851 census for the City of Toronto has been lost, there are some official records, at least, for every other year starting with 1797 for the Town of York. In 1799, for example, 23 Blacks are listed out of a total of 669 inhabitants, several clearly enslaved in Provincial Secretary William Jarvis's household. There were also unofficial counts of the urban population, and several of the city's Black population, that we can examine. A census is the only document that regularly identifies whether a person was Black or white. The 1851 census for York Township (the area outside the city) does survive. From that year forward, each census also gives the names of everyone living in the household, where they were born and what they did for a living, and other fascinating details, such as whether they could read and write, their religion, the type of house in which they lived, and whether or not they owned livestock. The census records can be found on the Library and Archives Canada website, and are searchable by name, location, and other details.

Another document that is very helpful is the *Toronto Street and Business Directory*. Starting in 1833, these books were like phone books without the phone numbers. There is usually a description of the city as it was at the time the directory was published, along with lists of government officials, names and locations of principal streets, locations of churches and public buildings, and the names of important organizations and associations. Directories then listed every householder in the city, where they lived and their occupations. Sometimes they also had the word *coloured* in brackets after a person's name, although this was not done consistently. Town of York Lists of Inhabitants and Toronto directories are all online at the Toronto Public Library website and make intriguing reading for anyone interested in the city's history.

Once someone's address has been found, more information is contained in the city tax assessment rolls. Some Toronto tax rolls also note whether people were of African origin and where they had been born. Chances are that someone listed as "Black" or "mulatto" (of mixed parentage) who had been born in Virginia or Kentucky had once been enslaved and perhaps came to Toronto on the Underground Railroad. Ontario tax assessment rolls are now digitized. They may be found at FamilySearch.org under "Ontario Tax Records 1834–1899."

Checking these documents against each other over a number of years can give an idea when people first arrived in the city, and perhaps when they either moved away or died. Checking cemetery records from the Toronto Necropolis and various churches is helpful because these give not only the exact date of death and the cause, but also identify the officiating minister and the person who purchased the burial plot. The websites of the Ontario Genealogical Society and the Toronto branch of the Ontario Genealogical Society are very helpful in this regard.

From this point, the sources for information can really vary quite widely. Most church baptismal, marriage, and death records for Toronto's early African Canadian churches have been lost, but Black families attending Anglican, Roman Catholic, or Presbyterian services had such important events recorded. Some of these are also available through FamilySearch.org, which is a free service.

School board records give the name of every child who went to city schools. These are preserved in the Toronto District School Board archives, although the ethnic background of the children was not noted. The records of students attending the Toronto Normal School (where teachers were trained), the various colleges of the University of Toronto, and private schools such as Upper Canada College are available. So are lists of Black men who served in the militia and in the army at various periods, including the Union Army in the Civil War.

Important families and those whose descendants are still living in Toronto have available collections of business and family papers, including letters, family Bibles, diaries, and photographs. The Anderson Ruffin Abbott Papers in the Toronto Reference Library's Baldwin Collection of Canadiana are a treasure trove. Historian Daniel G. Hill gathered copies of a large number of pictures and documents; the originals remain in private hands. The Daniel G. Hill Papers are divided between Library and Archives Canada and the Archives of Ontario. The

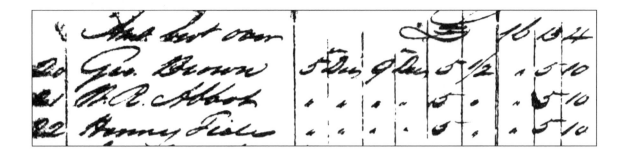

Wilson R. Abbott's enlistment in the Upper Canadian Militia, 1837 Rebellion.

latter also holds the very significant personal collection of Alvin McCurdy, an Amherstburg-area historian of African Canada, as well as the papers of Anglican Bishop John Strachan, where one version of the Gallego census of Toronto may be found. (The other is also in the Archives of Ontario, included in the Sydenham Papers.) Finally, there is the remarkable collection compiled by Wilma Morrison, who studied the history of Black people in the Niagara Falls area for more than half a century. These, too, are at the Archives of Ontario and include many clues to families who lived at one time in Toronto, or who had relatives there.

Black newspapers such as Henry Bibb's *Voice of the Fugitive* and Mary Ann Shadd's *Provincial Freeman* are invaluable resources for the study of this topic. Other Toronto newspapers such as the *Colonial Advocate*, the *Leader*, and the *Patriot* expressed opinions on the larger events of the day, while George Brown's *Globe* was a strong and constant voice supporting the antislavery struggle. The Toronto *World* is useful for the latter part of the nineteenth century. All these are available on microfilm at the Toronto Reference Library. The *Voice of the Fugitive* and *Provincial Freeman* are available online through the INK-ODW Newspaper Collection.

Finally, the Ontario Black History Society has for many years gathered together information about the history of African Canadians living in this province. A great deal of the materials in the OBHS collection has been donated by families and individuals whose ancestors were freedom seekers and free Black immigrants in the nineteenth century.

# twelve

# HOW DO WE KNOW? ARCHAEOLOGY

ARCHAEOLOGY HELPS US learn about our city's rich African Canadian past. Archaeologists carefully dig through layers of soil that have built up over the years at places people once worked or lived. These are called "archaeological sites." Excavating such sites helps us learn more about what human beings did there at each period of the site's history. Each layer represents an era in the life of the site, the top layer being the most recent. Digging a site is like going back in time.

Historical archaeologists also seek out clues in old documents such as census, tax and church records, newspapers, letters, diaries, and maps. Combined with objects people made or used in the past (artifacts) along with the remains of foundation walls, wells, and even old outhouses (outdoor toilets), documentary evidence can help archaeologists understand more about the daily lives of people who came to Toronto in the Underground Railroad era.

Toronto is very built-up, but important archaeological sites still lie under parking lots, parks, and playgrounds. When archaeologists locate such sites, they first lay out a grid of squares or trenches so they can carefully measure and map the exact location of each of their discoveries. Then they carefully remove and sift each layer of soil. Everything is photographed, because excavators destroy their sites as they dig. They do this by taking away the soil layers that have built up over each period of time in which people lived, or worked, or even just visited that particular site.

Archaeologists and other specialists collect the artifacts and study them in light of other types of data they have recovered. Seeds can help us understand what people grew and ate in the past. Animal and fish bones tell us what they hunted to help them survive. Buttons indicate what types of clothing they may have worn. Household dishes, cutlery, and tools suggest how they may have managed their homes, gardens, and businesses.

## THE HOME OF LUCIE AND THORNTON BLACKBURN

The first Underground Railroad site dug in Canada was the home of Kentucky freedom seekers Thornton and Lucie Blackburn. They started Toronto's first taxi business. With support from the Toronto school board, the provincial government, and the Ontario Black History Society, in 1985, Karolyn Smardz Frost and her team found the Blackburn Site. It was located under the playground of what is now Inglenook Community School in Toronto's east end near the mouth of the Don River.

The couple lived on Eastern Avenue from 1834 until their deaths in the 1890s. Since the Blackburns had not been allowed to learn to read or write while enslaved in the South, they left no record of their experiences in their own words. Soon after they died their home and barn/stable were torn down. The buildings' foundations and the hundreds of artifacts the Blackburns left behind lay buried until 1985, when the archaeological team brought them again to light.

Three thousand school children helped dig the Blackburn site, and tens of thousands of people came to visit. Everyone was excited by the discovery of a number of children's toys under the floorboards of Lucie and Thornton's modest wooden bungalow. This was a mystery, for the couple had no children. However,

old newspapers name the Blackburns as donors to the antislavery cause. Archaeologists now believe that the Blackburns sometimes invited newly arrived freedom seekers to stay at their own home. Some of their guests had children, such as Ann Maria Jackson's little boy, Albert Jackson, aged two, who would grow up to become Toronto's first Black postman.

The Blackburns' house was a common type in the American South. Called a "shotgun house," its foundations showed it was long and narrow, with three rooms set in a row. The front room facing the street was the living room, and the middle room behind it served as the bedroom. The kitchen stood at the back, looking over the Blackburns' large garden and fruit trees. In the corner was a brick fireplace and chimney where they cooked. Bones of ducks, rabbits, and fish were found there.

Under the bedroom floor, archaeologists discovered a deep, earth-lined cellar filled with bricks and debris. There they found a treasure trove of household goods, such as preserving jars, cutlery,

(top left) Thornton and Lucie Blackburn Site, 1985.

(top right) Students excavating at the Thornton and Lucie Blackburn Site, 1985.

(bottom) Artifacts in the ground and trowel, Thornton and Lucie Blackburn Site.

Hand-dug root cellar beneath the former bedroom of Thornton and Lucie Blackburn, showing layers of dirt and debris, including bricks from the chimney thrown into the pit when the house was demolished.

glassware, and broken china. Such cellars are a legacy of slavery and are often discovered when archaeologists excavate Southern plantations. Beneath the floors of cabins where they were forced to live, enslaved people used secret cellars to hide precious items and extra food for their families.

The Blackburn barn stood right next to the street. The upper floor was a hayloft, and the horse that pulled the Blackburn cab was stabled below. The red and yellow carriage that served as their taxi was stored at the other end of the building. Burned into the earthen floor was the outline of an anvil, where a blacksmith once had a fire so he could shoe Thornton and Lucie's horses. Behind the buildings was a larger burned area where Lucie and her husband used to dispose of their garbage.

## THE COURTHOUSE SITE

Thirty years after the Blackburn dig, archaeologists hired by Infrastructure Ontario found another site important to Toronto's Underground Railroad history. They excavated a whole city block north of Osgoode Hall, behind Toronto City Hall. In 2015, archaeologist Holly Martelle and her team from Timmins Martelle Heritage Consultants removed the paving of a parking lot to expose foundations of many homes and businesses. The British Methodist Episcopal Church and some of the other buildings there had been constructed by African American immigrants who came to Canada in search of freedom before the U.S. Civil War.

This was a very old and complicated site, with many overlapping and intersecting walls and other features. First Nations people lived in that area for more

Foundations of the British Methodist Episcopal Church on Sayre (Chestnut) Street in St. John's Ward, Courthouse Site.

than twelve thousand years. They were the first people to leave artifacts behind at this site. Sadly, other traces of their activities had been obliterated by many phases of building and rebuilding in later centuries. The lands on which Toronto now stands were obtained by British colonizers in 1788 from the First Nations in the area. This was the so-called Toronto Purchase. The agreement was found to be very unfair and not legally binding. First in 1805 and then again in 1998 new agreements were made, the latter for $145 million. It was the largest land claim settlement ever made in Canada at the time.

In 1793, British colonizers arrived to establish the "Town of York" as the provincial capital of Upper Canada. They cut down thousands of trees and laid out a grid of streets east of Yonge Street and south of King. In 1834, Toronto became a city and regained its proper First Nations' name. As Toronto's population grew, the area west of Yonge and north of Queen Street was measured out and sold off in small, inexpensive house lots.

Archaeologists at the Courthouse Site were excavating part of Toronto's first working-class neighbourhood. The block was home to wave after wave of immigrants, starting in the 1830s. Freedom seekers and free African Americans who came to Toronto in the era of the Underground Railroad found their first Toronto homes here. So did their neighbours from England, Ireland, and Scotland. They established homes and businesses in St. Patrick's Ward, which stretched from Yonge Street almost to Spadina. The part of St. Patrick's Ward that lay between Yonge and University as far north as Bloor was renamed St. John's Ward in 1852.

St. John's Ward was a close-knit community centred around home, church, and family. A small wood-framed church was built here in 1845 by Black families. In 1856 it became the British Methodist Episcopal Church, a newly established African Canadian denomination. The area was home to the first Canadian-born Black doctor, Dr. Anderson Ruffin Abbott, and to many artisans and craftspeople. Mrs. Frances Teakle was a widow who owned two confectionary shops, Virginia-born Charles Peyton Lucas was a blacksmith, and John M. Tinsley owned a successful construction company where many freedom seekers found employment.

In the years after Confederation, many African Canadians and their neighbours moved on to other parts of the expanding city. The houses in which they used to live were bought as investments and rental property, and new landlords let them deteriorate. Wave after wave of immigrants rented or bought homes on these narrow streets. Eastern Europeans, most of them Jewish, moved in to work and raise their families. A good many were poor, and the area came to be known as only "The Ward." Italians and other European immigrants settled there around the turn of the twentieth century. Later, Chinese people bought homes and started shops and restaurants. Each resident of these modest homes left artifacts and other clues behind in the soil over more than 185 years of occupation.

Archaeology helps show the types of discrimination African Torontonians faced in the city they had adopted as their home. One of the local residents owned a ceramic figurine representing a "minstrel" playing a banjo. It represents the deeply racist minstrel shows that were popular entertainments in Canada starting in the mid-nineteenth century and continuing through the 1960s. These were the same blackface performances that Wilson Ruffin Abbott and so many members of Toronto's Black community had petitioned City Hall to prohibit starting in 1840.

One of the houses excavated in 2015 was that of Cecelia Jane Reynolds, who had escaped Kentucky slavery at age fifteen. Her story is told elsewhere in this book. Next door was a house built by shoemaker Francis Griffin Simpson. He eventually bought Cecelia's house, and a large cache of old leather and half-made shoes was found in the two yards. Nearby lived barber Edward Jones, whose little girl very likely treasured the special doll with a black-glazed ceramic head pictured in chapter 7 of this book. It was made in Germany especially for African American and African Canadian children. Another local resident owned the beautiful soup plate transfer printed with the famous scene of Eliza crossing the Ohio from the landmark anti-slavery novel *Uncle Tom's Cabin* (1851) by Harriet Beecher Stowe.

Foundation of the home Cecelia Jane Reynolds shared with her Underground Railroad conductor husband Benjamin Pollard Holmes. Courthouse Site in St. John's Ward.

# ACKNOWLEDGEMENTS

THIS BOOK IS MORE THAN a labour of love. Many people have heard of the Underground Railroad that brought thousands of freedom seekers to Canada, but very few know that Toronto was an important terminus of those secret routes. For the purposes of this volume we use the term *Underground Railroad* to identify the population movement that brought African Americans to Canada in the years before the American Civil War. Today we realize that half or more of those who broke their own chains and sought liberty in British North America did so with little or no assistance. We also note that an uncounted number of African Americans who became African Canadians were free people who migrated northward seeking better lives for themselves and their children.

*The Underground Railroad: Next Stop, Toronto!* is indebted to the work of earlier researchers and authors. We owe a debt to Dr. Daniel Hill, president emeritus of the Ontario Black History Society, who wrote several seminal articles on the history of Blacks in Toronto, in addition to his well-known book *The Freedom-Seekers: Blacks in Early Canada* (1981). These articles are known only to a small coterie of researchers and historians, but they and the work of other earlier historians have been enormously important to our studies. In the area of African

Canadian history, we also recognize the landmark contributions of Dr. James W. St. G. Walker and the role he has played as a mentor to us in our scholarship over the years. *The Underground Railroad: Next Stop, Toronto!* builds on the efforts of Dr. Hill, Dr. Walker, and others to bring to public attention a great deal of new and highly significant information regarding Toronto's African Canadian past. For that we are immensely grateful.

As always, there are many fortuitous events that magically come together to give birth to the "baby." The information contained in this book was gathered over the course of a two-year research project conducted in 2001–2 to produce the experiential theatre production *The Underground Railroad: Next Stop, Freedom.* Part of the Historic Sites and Monuments Board of Canada's initiative to recognize sites connected with the Underground Railroad, it opened at the Royal Ontario Museum in the fall of 2002. The associated travelling exhibit made the rounds of Canadian museums and historical societies for nearly two decades before finding a permanent home in the Oakville Museum at the Erchless Estate.

The Ontario Black History Society has been our stalwart friend and supporter throughout, and special appreciation is due to president Natasha Henry, vice-presidents Channon Oyeniran and Mawuli Chai, treasurer Dorothy Abbott, secretary Amani Ausar, executive director Michele-Ann Halsall, co-ordinator Pam Houston, and all the members at large. We also acknowledge here the leadership and landmark effort of our dear friend, the Honourable Jean Augustine. A former school superintendent, she was the first African Canadian woman elected to the House of Commons, serving for seventeen years in many important offices including secretary of state for multiculturalism. She was the first person of African descent to sit as deputy speaker of the House. Dr. Augustine's concern for children's education and profound love of Black history shine through in all she does.

We take this opportunity to thank the original consultative committee for "The Underground Railroad: Next Stop, Freedom" project: Rosemary Sadlier, then president of the Ontario Black History Society; Daniel O'Brien of the Ontario Ministry of Culture; Christine Lockett of the Royal Ontario Museum;

Superintendent of Education Madge Logan and historian and freedom seeker descendant Catherine Slaney; Toronto filmmaker, actor, and author Anthony Sherwood; and the Parks Canada staff members, who so ably steered the original project out of which our research for this book came. All retired now, it was our colleagues from Parks Canada who generously permitted us to share here the discoveries we made in the course of our research: Ross Thompson, Southwestern Ontario Field Unit superintendent; Rob Watt, project manager; historians Owen Thomas and Shannon Ricketts; and curator Derek Cooke. We would also like to thank Tom Lackey for a terrific script, and exhibit designers Steve and Claudette Shaw of Steve Shaw Productions for their tireless efforts and professionalism in producing the exhibit.

We are grateful to numerous individuals and archival repositories for permission to include their photographic and other visual materials in this publication: Dr. Daniel G. and Donna Hill; the First Baptist Church, Toronto; the Art and Research Resources departments at Library and Archives Canada; the late Donald Nethery, Toronto District School Board Museum and Archives; Karen Teeple, City of Toronto Archives; the Market Gallery, Toronto; Trinity College Archives, University of Toronto; Special Collections, Toronto Reference Library; the Bentley Historical Library, University of Michigan; the Archives of Ontario, Toronto; the McCord Museum, Montreal; the Chicago History Museum; Canada Post Corporation; and the Ontario Black History Society. The images enhance tremendously the quality and appeal of the text. For this most recent edition, a note of thanks goes to Infrastructure Ontario and also to principal archaeologist and heritage planner Holly Martelle and material culturalist Nicole Brandon of Timmins Martelle Heritage Consultants for kindly sharing with us some of the unpublished artifact and site photos from the Courthouse Site in Toronto.

The contributions made to our volume by genealogist extraordinaire Guylaine Pétrin are very much appreciated. She has been unfailingly generous in sharing her wealth of knowledge with us. We are also grateful to Sally Gibson of the

Cabbagetown Historical Society for allowing us to reference her remarkable discovery that the image on page 40 includes the first known photograph taken of an African Canadian woman in Toronto.

We are forever indebted to Jane Gibson and Barry Penhale, the former publishers of Natural Heritage Books, for their interest and dedication to ensuring that the original edition of *The Underground Railroad: Next Stop, Toronto!* was brought to the public. Without their vision, the first edition of this book might never have seen the light of day. The Penhales remain good friends to us and continue to make their unique and very significant contributions to history and culture in their Grey-Bruce home.

At Dundurn Press, publisher Scott Fraser, associate publisher Kathryn Lane, and managing editor Elena Radic enthusiastically embraced the idea of publishing this new and updated edition. *The Underground Railroad: Next Stop, Toronto!* remains, to date, the only book providing a detailed overview of Toronto's rich nineteenth-century African Canadian past. We appreciate the work of everyone involved in designing, printing, and disseminating this edition and look forward to sharing its contents with the world. Thanks, too, go to literary agent Michael Levine, president of the Westwood Agency, who saw the importance of publishing a new edition and applied his considerable energies and creativity to bringing this project to fruition.

Afua Cooper and Karolyn Smardz Frost would like to add a special note of thanks to our co-author, Adrienne Shadd. To a large extent it was her meticulous attention to detail and her commitment to excellence that made this new edition possible. We want Adrienne to know how much we appreciate all the effort she has put in to bringing this updated and redesigned version of *The Underground Railroad: Next Stop, Toronto!* to a new generation of readers.

As always, we acknowledge and thank our families — Marishana, Alyson, Lauren, Brandon, Nathan, Habiba, Lamarana, Akil, Norm, Jamie, Sara, Graham, Hannah, Oliver, Jason, Karina, Max, and Sawyer — for their patience and unending support.

# NOTES

## Introduction

1. Benjamin Drew, *The Refugee: Or The Narratives of Fugitive Slaves in Canada* (Boston, 1856), 94.
2. The Fugitive Slave Law, passed by the American government in 1850, expanded the ability of the government to protect the interests of slaveholders. This law required the capture and return to their owners of all freedom seekers, even those who had escaped the South and made it all the way to the Northern states.
3. According to Statistics Canada, in 2016 Canada had almost 1.2 million Black people and 442,015 or 37 percent lived in Toronto. See "Diversity of the Black Population in Canada: An Overview" at www150.statcan.gc.ca/n1/daily-quotidien/190227/dq190227d-eng.htm.

## Chapter 2: Blacks in Early Toronto

1. Edith G. Firth, *The Town of York, 1793, 1815: A Collection of Documents of Early Toronto*, vol. 1 (Toronto: University of Toronto Press, 1962), lxxviii.
2. John Steckley, "Toronto … or is that Taranteau," in *Explore Historic Toronto*, Toronto Historical Board, November 1992. See also toronto.ca/311/knowledgebase/kb/docs/articles/311-toronto/information-and-business-development/origin-of-the-name-of-toronto.html.

## Chapter 3: Underground Railroad to Toronto

1. This story appears in W.M. Mitchell, *The Underground Rail Road*, 2nd ed. (London: William Tweedie, 1860), 11–12.

2. Although many sources state that Harriet Tubman made nineteen trips to the South, rescuing hundreds of people, recent scholarship shows that these statistics come from a Tubman biography written by Sarah Bradford in 1869. Harriet herself stated in 1858 or 1859 that she had made fewer than ten trips up to that point, rescuing between fifty and sixty people. Kate Clifford Larson, whose landmark volume *Bound for the Promised Land: Harriet Tubman, Portrait of an American Hero* represents years of scholarly detective work, stated in an article for the *Washington Post*, "My research has confirmed that estimate, establishing that she brought away about 70 people in about 13 trips and gave instructions to about 70 more who found their way to freedom on their own." See Kate Clifford Larson, "Five Myths About Harriet Tubman," *Washington Post*, April 22, 2016; and Miriam Fauzia, "Fact Check: Harriet Tubman Helped Free Slaves for the Underground Railroad, But Not 300," *USA Today*, July 21, 2020.

3. From 1791 to 1841, the Province of Ontario was known as Upper Canada. Between 1841 and 1867, it was called Canada West. In 1867, the year of Canada's Confederation, it became Ontario.

## Chapter 9: Black Torontonians in the Civil War

1. In the last two decades of the nineteenth century and the early decades of the twentieth, American states began enacting laws that solidified what came to be known as "segregation." Black people were no longer permitted to share railway cars, streetcars, and buses, public washrooms, theatres, restaurants, schools, and other public facilities with white people. It was only in the 1960s, with the rise of the Civil Rights Movement, that these harsh and restrictive laws were removed. They were called Jim Crow laws because of a famous character from the 1830s — a white actor who blackened his face with shoe polish or lamp blacking and danced and sang, pretending to be a happy, silly Southern slave. This very insulting stereotype came to be used as the title for all repressive laws and customs that white Americans imposed on Black Americans.

# FURTHER READING

Alexander, Ken, and Avis Glaze. *Towards Freedom: The African Canadian Experience.* Toronto: Umbrella Press, 1996.

Armstrong, F.H. *Toronto: The Place of Meeting.* Toronto: Windsor Publications, 1993.

———. "The Toronto Directories and the Negro Community in the Late 1840s." *Ontario History* 61, no. 2 (June 1969): 111–19.

Bordowich, Fergus. *Bound for Canaan: The Epic Story of the Underground Railroad, America's First Civil Rights Movement.* New York: HarperCollins, 2005.

Bristow, Peggy, Dionne Brand, Linda Carty, Afua Cooper, Sylvia Hamilton, and Adrienne Shadd. *"We're Rooted Here and They Can't Pull Us Up": Essays in African Canadian Women's History.* Toronto: University of Toronto Press, 1994.

Brode, Patrick. *The Odyssey of John Anderson Toronto.* Published for the Osgoode Society. Toronto: University of Toronto Press, 1989.

Calarco, Tom. *People of the Underground Railroad: A Biographical Dictionary.* Westport, CT: Greenwood Press, 2008.

Calarco, Tom, et al. *Places of the Underground Railroad: A Geographical Guide.* Santa Barbara, CA: ABC-CLIO, 2011.

Cooper, Afua. *The Hanging of Angelique: The Untold Story of Canadian Slavery and the Burning of Old Montreal.* Toronto: HarperCollins, 2006.

Dawson, Hilary. "From Immigrant to Establishment: A Black Family's Journey." *Ontario History* (Ontario Historical Society) 99, no. 1 (Spring 2007): 31–43.

Drew, Benjamin. *The Refugee; or, The Narrative of Fugitive Slaves in Canada*. Boston: 1854. Reprinted with introduction by George Elliott Clarke. Toronto: Dundurn Press, 2008.

Elgersman, Maureen. *Unyielding Spirits: Black Women and Slavery in Early Canada and Jamaica*. New York: Garland Publishing, 1999.

Firth, Edith, ed. *The Town of York, A Collection of Documents of Early Toronto*. Vol. 5 of the Ontario Series, Champlain Society. Toronto: University of Toronto Press, 1952.

Foner, Eric. *Gateway to Freedom: The Hidden History of the Underground Railroad*. New York: W.W. Norton, 2015.

Henry, Natasha. *Emancipation Day: Celebrating Freedom in Canada*. Toronto: Dundurn Press, 2010.

Hill, Daniel G. "The Blacks in Toronto," in *Gathering Place: Peoples and Neighbourhoods of Toronto, 1834–1945,* Robert F. Harney, ed. Toronto: Multicultural History Society of Ontario, 1985: 75–105.

———. *The Freedom-Seekers: Blacks in Early Canada*. Agincourt: The Book Society of Canada, 1981. Reprint, Toronto: Stoddard, 2004.

———."Negroes in Toronto, 1793–1865." *Ontario History* 55, no. 2 (1963): 73–91.

Hill, Lawrence. *Any Known Blood*. Toronto: HarperCollins Canada, 1997.

———. *Women of Vision: Canadian Negro Women's Association 1951–1976*. Toronto: Umbrella Press, 1996.

Hubbard, Stephen. *Against All Odds: The Story of William Peyton Hubbard, Black Leader and Municipal Reformer*. Toronto: Dundurn Press, 1987.

Hudson, J. Blaine: *Encyclopedia of the Underground Railroad*. Jefferson, NC: McFarland Publishing, 2006.

Jackson, Ruby West, and Walter T. McDonald. *Finding Freedom: The Untold Story of Joshua Glover, Runaway Slave*. Madison: Wisconsin Historical Society Press, 2007.

Larson, Kate Clifford. *Bound for the Promised Land: Harriet Tubman. Portrait of an American Hero*. New York: Ballantine Books, 2004.

Lorinc, John, Michael McClelland, Ellen Scheinberg, and Tatum Taylor. *The Ward: The Life and Loss of Toronto's First Immigrant Neighbourhood*. Toronto: Coach House Books, 2015.

Martell, Holly, Michael McClelland, Tatum Taylor, and John Lorinc. *The Ward Uncovered: The Archaeology of Everyday Life*. Toronto: Coach House Books, 2018.

Mathieu, Sarah-Jane. *North of the Colour Line: Migration and Black Resistance*. Chapel Hill: University of North Carolina Press, 2010.

Meyler, Peter, ed. *Broken Shackles: Old Man Henson from Slavery to Freedom*. Toronto: Dundurn Press, 2007. New ed. of John Frost [Glenelg, pseud.], *Broken Shackles*, first published Toronto, 1889.

Meyler, Peter, and David Meyler. *A Stolen Life: Searching for Richard Pierpoint*. Toronto: Dundurn Press, 1999.

Mitchell, Rev. William M. *The Under-Ground Railroad*. London: Wm. Tweedie, 1860.

Newby, M. Dalyce. *Anderson Ruffin Abbott: First Afro-Canadian Doctor*. Markham, ON: Associated Medical Services/Fitzhenry & Whiteside, 1998.

Pétrin, Guylaine. "The Myth of Mary Mink: Representation of Black Women in Toronto in the Nineteenth Century." *Ontario History* 108, no. 1 (Spring 2016): 92–110.

Rhodes, Jane. *Mary Ann Shadd Cary: The Black Press and Protest in the Nineteenth Century*. Bloomington: University of Indiana Press, 1998.

Ripley, C. Peter, ed. *The Black Abolitionist Papers*. Vol. 2, *Canada, 1830–1865*. Chapel Hill: University of North Carolina Press, 1986.

Robinson, David, and Douglas Smith. *Sources of the African Past*. New York: Africana Publishing, 1979.

Scadding, Henry. *Toronto of Old: Collections and Recollections*. Toronto: Adam, Stevenson, 1873. Reprint, F.H. Armstrong, ed., Toronto: Dundurn Press,1987.

Shadd, Adrienne. *The Journey from Tollgate to Parkway: African Canadians in Hamilton*. Toronto: Dundurn Press, 2010.

Siebert, Wilbur. *The Underground Railroad from Slavery to Freedom*. New York: Macmillan, 1898. Reprint, New York: Arno Press, 1968.

Silverman, Jason. *Unwelcome Guests: The White Canadian Response to American Fugitive Slaves, 1860–1865*. New York: Associated Faculty Press, 1985.

Simpson, Donald. *Under the North Star: Black Communities in Canada*. Paul E. Lovejoy, ed. Trenton, NJ: Africa World Press, 2005.

Slaney, Catherine. *Family Secrets: Crossing the Colour Line*. Toronto: Dundurn, 2003.

Smallwood, Thomas. *A Narrative of Thomas Smallwood (Coloured Man 1851)*. Toronto: James Stephens, privately printed, 1851. Reprint, Richard Almonte, ed., Toronto: Mercury Press, 2000.

Smardz Frost, Karolyn. *I've Got a Home in Glory Land: A Lost Tale of the Underground Railroad*. Toronto: Dundurn Press and New York: Farrar Straus Giroux, 2007.

———. *Steal Away Home: One Woman's Epic Flight to Freedom — And Her Long Road Back to the South*. Toronto: HarperCollins Canada, 2017.

Smardz Frost, Karolyn, Bryan Walls, Frederick H. Armstrong, and Hilary Bates Neary, eds. *Ontario's African-Canadian Heritage: Collected Writings by Fred Landon, 1918–1967*. Toronto: Dundurn Press, 2009.

Still, William. *The Underground Rail Road*. Philadelphia: Porter and Coates, 1872. Reprint, Chicago: Johnson Publishing, 1970.

Stouffer, Allen. *The Light of Nature and the Law of God: Antislavery in Ontario 1833–1877*. Baton Rouge: Louisiana State University Press, 1992.

Walker, James W. St. G. *A History of Blacks in Canada: A Study Guide for Teachers and Students*. Hull, QC: Minister of State, Multiculturalism, 1980.

Ward, Samuel Ringgold. *Autobiography of a Fugitive Negro: His Anti-Slavery Labors in the United States, Canada & England*. London: James Snow, 1855. Reprint, Chicago: Johnson Publishing, 1970.

Wayne, Michael. "The Myth of the Fugitive Slave: The Black Population of Canada West on the Eve of the Civil War." *L'Histoire Sociale/Social History* 28, no. 56 (November 1995): 465–81.

Winks, Robin. *The Blacks in Canada: A History*. 2nd ed. Montreal: McGill-Queen's University Press, 2005.

## Suggestions for Junior Readers

Ayres, Katherine. *North By Night: A Story of the Underground Railroad*. New York: Delacorte Press, 1998.

Badoe, Adwoa. *The Pot of Wisdom*: *Ananse Stories*. Toronto: Groundwood Books, 2008.

Bradford, Karleen. *A Desperate Road to Freedom: The Underground Railroad Diary of Julia May Jackson, Virginia to Canada West, 1863–1864*. Toronto: Scholastic Press, 2012.

Carbone, Elisa. *Stealing Freedom*. New York: Knopf, 1998.

Cooper, Afua. *My Name is Henry Bibb*: *A Story of Slavery and Freedom*. Toronto: Kids Can Press, 2009.

Gillard, Denise, with Stephen Taylor. *Music from the Sky*. Toronto: Douglass and McIntyre, 2001.

Girard, Linda. *Young Frederick Douglass*. Illinois: Modern Grove Press, 1994.

Gorrell, Gena K. *The Story of the Underground Railroad*. Toronto: Stoddart Publishing, 1996.

Granfield, Linda. *Amazing Grace: The Story of the Hymn*. Toronto: Tundra Books, 1997.

Greenwood, Barbara. *The Last Safe House: A Story of the Underground Railroad*. Toronto: Kids Can Press, 1998.

Haskins, James, and Kathleen Benson. *Building a New Land: African Americans in Colonial America*. New York: HarperCollins, 2001.

Henry, Natasha. *Coming Together*. Oakville, ON: Rubicon Publishing, 2022.

———. *Talking about Freedom: Celebrating Emancipation Day in Canada*. Toronto: Dundurn Press, 2012.

Henry, Natasha, ed. *African Diaspora*. Oakville, ON: Rubicon Publishing, 2015.

———. *Firsts*. Oakville, ON: Rubicon Publishing, 2014.

Hill, Lawrence. *Beatrice and Croc Harry*. Toronto: HarperCollins, 2022.

———. *Trials and Triumphs: The Story of African Canadians*. Toronto: Umbrella Press, 1993.

Jenkins, Earnestine. *A Glorious Past: Ancient Egypt Ethiopia and Nubia*. New York: Chelsea House, 1995.

Krass, Peter. *Sojourner Truth, Anti-Slavery Activist*. Los Angeles: Melrose Square Publishing, 1988.

Lemelle, Sid. *Pan Africanism for Beginners*. New York: Writers and Readers, 1992.

McKissack, Patricia. *Nzingha, Warrior Queen of Matamba*. New York: Scholastic, 2000.

Paulsen, Gary. *Nightjohn*. New York: Delacourt Press, 1993.

Prince, Bryan. *I Came as a Stranger: The Underground Railroad*. Toronto: Tundra Books, 2004.

Ringgold, Faith. *Aunt Harriet's Underground Railroad in the Sky*. New York: Crown Publishers, 1992.

Sadlier, Rosemary. *The Kids' Book of Black Canadian History*. Toronto: Kids Can Press, 2003.

———. *Mary Ann Shadd: Publisher-Editor-Teacher-Lawyer-Suffragette*. Toronto: Umbrella Press, 1995.

———. *Tubman: Harriet Tubman and the Underground Railroad*. Toronto: Umbrella Press, 1997.

Schroeder, Alan, and Jerry Pinckney. *Minty: A Story of Young Harriet Tubman*. New York: Dial Books for Young Readers, 1996.

Schwam, Virginia Frances. *Crossing to Freedom*. Toronto: Scholastic, 2010.

———. *If I Just Had Two Wings*. Toronto: Fitzhenry and Whiteside, 2001.

Shadd, Adrienne, ed. *Early Civilizations of Africa*. Oakville, ON: Rubicon Publishing, 2015.

_____. *Freedom*. Oakville, ON: Rubicon Publishing, 2014.
Winter, Jeanette. *Follow the Drinking Gourd*. New York: Knopf, 1998.
Wisniewski, David. *Sundiata: Lion King of Mali*. New York: Clarion Books, 1992.
Wright, Courtney C. *Jumping the Broom*. New York: Holiday House, 1994.

## Selected Poetry for the Young Reader

Brand, Dionne. *Earth Magic*. Toronto: Sister Vision Press, 1993.
Cooper, Afua. *The Red Caterpillar on College Street*. Toronto: Sister Vision Press, 1989.
Rochelle, Brenda. *Words with Wings: A Treasury of African American Poetry and Art*. New York: HarperCollins, 2001.

# IMAGE CREDITS

27    From William Still, *The Underground Rail Road* (Philadelphia: Porter & Coates, 1872), 302.

29    Courtesy of Bentley Historical Library, University of Michigan.

30    From William Still, *The Underground Rail Road* (Philadelphia: Porter & Coates, 1872), opp. 125.

31    From William Still, *The Underground Rail Road* (Philadelphia: Porter & Coates, 1872), frontispiece.

32    Courtesy of Toronto Public Library (TRL), J.V. Salmon Collection, S1-960.

34    Courtesy of the City of Toronto Archives, Series 1465, File 119, Item 47.

35    Photo by Adrienne Shadd.

36    Courtesy of Toronto Public Library (TRL), T33461.

39    Courtesy of Archives of Ontario, McCurdy Collection, AO 5442.

40    Photo by Armstrong, Beere, and Hime. Courtesy of the City of Toronto Archives, Fonds 1498, Item 17.

42    From Goad's *Atlas of the City of Toronto* (Toronto: 1884), Sheet # 9. Courtesy of Map and Data Library, University of Toronto Libraries.

44    Courtesy of the City of Toronto Archives, Series 372, Subseries 55, Item 49.

45    From the *Provincial Freeman*, October 28, 1854.

46    Courtesy of the City of Toronto Archives, RG8 Series 14, Vol. 1A, Item 11.

48    Courtesy of Toronto Public Library (TRL), J. Ross Robertson Collection, T 12178.

49    Courtesy of Toronto Public Library (TRL), T 11049.

52    Courtesy of Library and Archives Canada.

54    Photo by Adrienne Shadd.

56    Photo by Stuart Logan Thompson. Toronto Public Library (TRL) T33468.

58    Courtesy of Infrastructure Ontario and Holly Martelle, Timmins Martelle Heritage Consultants.

| | |
|---|---|
| 60 | Courtesy of the City of Toronto Culture Division, Market Gallery Art Collection, A85-5. |
| 61 (top & bottom) | Courtesy of Infrastructure Ontario and Holly Martelle, Timmins Martelle Heritage Consultants. |
| 63 | Courtesy of Toronto Public Library (TRL), T 14120. |
| 64 | From Samuel Ringgold Ward, *Autobiography of a Fugitive Negro: His Anti-Slavery Labors in the United States, Canada, and England* (London, U.K.: John Snow, 1855), frontispiece. |
| 66 | Courtesy of City of Toronto Archives Series 372, Subseries 52, Item 794. |
| 67 | Courtesy of Toronto Public Library (TRL), PICTURES-R-3951. |
| 68 (top) | From Henry Bibb, *Narrative of the Life and Adventures of Henry Bibb, an American Slave* (New York: Henry Bibb, 1849), frontispiece. |
| 68 (bottom) | From *Voice of the Fugitive*, March 26, 1851. |
| 71 | Courtesy of the McCord Museum, William Notman, I-0.55.1. |
| 72 | Photo by Adrienne Shadd. |
| 74 | Courtesy of Toronto Public Library (TRL), Abbott Papers, S90 no. 37. |
| 77 | Courtesy of Library and Archives Canada, the Daniel Hill Collection, PA 211254. |
| 78 | Courtesy of the Chicago History Museum, ICHi-008058. |
| 79 | Courtesy of the Chicago History Museum, ICHi-007784. |
| 80 | Courtesy of Library and Archives Canada, the Daniel Hill Collection, PA 211257. |
| 80 (inset) | Courtesy of Library and Archives Canada, the Daniel Hill Collection, PA 211255. |
| 83 | Courtesy of Library and Archives Canada, the Daniel Hill Collection, PA 211251. |
| 84 | From *Rowsell's City of Toronto and County of York Directory, for 1850-51* (Toronto: Rowsell, 1850), 60. |
| 86 | From *Globe*, October 17, 1860, 4. |
| 88 | From John Ross Robertson, *Landmarks of Toronto*, Vol. 2 (Toronto: J. Ross Robertson, 1896), 677–78. |

| | |
|---|---|
| 89 | From Reverend W.M. Mitchell, *The Under-Ground Railroad* (London, U.K.: William Tweedie, 1860), frontispiece. |
| 90 | Courtesy of Infrastructure Ontario and Holly Martelle, Timmins Martelle Heritage Consultants. |
| 92 | From *Provincial Freeman*, July 8, 1854. |
| 94 | Courtesy of Library and Archives Canada, C29977. |
| 95 | From *Provincial Freeman*, November 11, 1854. |
| 96 (left) | From William Still, *The Underground Rail Road* (Philadelphia: Porter & Coates, 1872), 512. |
| 96 (right) | Courtesy of Canada Post Corporation, 2019. |
| 98 | Courtesy of Infrastructure Ontario and Holly Martelle, Timmins Martelle Heritage Consultants. |
| 99 | From *Provincial Freeman*, October 13, 1855. |
| 100 | From *Thomas Smallwood, A Narrative of Thomas Smallwood (Coloured Man)* (Toronto: Thomas Smallwood, 1851. Reprinted in Toronto by Mercury Press, 2000, Richard Almonte, ed.). Used with permission of Mercury Press. |
| 102 (top & bottom) | Courtesy of Infrastructure Ontario and Holly Martelle, Timmins Martelle Heritage Consultants. |
| 104 | Courtesy of City of Toronto Archives, TTC Fonds, Series 71, Item 10179. |
| 108 | Courtesy of Library and Archives Canada, Detachments, Unembodied Regiments, Militia Service –Upper Canada, File WO 13/3677. |
| 111 (top left) | Photo by Christopher Koch. |
| 111 (top right) | Photo by Duncan Scherberger. |
| 111 (bottom) | Photo by Christopher Koch. |
| 112 | Photo by Christopher Koch. |
| 113 | Courtesy of Infrastructure Ontario and Holly Martelle, Timmins Martelle Heritage Consultants. |
| 115 | Courtesy of Infrastructure Ontario and Holly Martelle, Timmins Martelle Heritage Consultants. |

# INDEX

# ABOUT THE AUTHORS

**Adrienne Shadd** is a consultant, curator, and author who has conducted research for plaques, films, and exhibits, including "I'll Use My Freedom Well," the exhibit at Uncle Tom's Cabin, and Black Mecca: The Story of Chatham's Black Community. Most recently she has collaborated on the Black heritage of "The Ward" neighbourhood for installation at the new courthouse just north of Osgoode Hall, Toronto. She is the author, co-author, and editor of numerous books and articles, including *The Journey from Tollgate to Parkway: African Canadians in Hamilton* and *Talking About Identity: Encounters in Race, Ethnicity, and Language*, with Carl James. She has also collaborated on the award-winning children's publication *Freedom*, and *Early Civilizations of Africa*, both of the Sankofa Black Heritage Collection, with Rubicon Publishing. Adrienne has been recognized with the William P. Hubbard Award for Race Relations and the J.C. Holland Award for Arts Achievement for her research and writing. She is currently working on a book on Toronto settler and freedom seeker Deborah Brown, and is Senior Historian, Special Projects, for A Black People's History of Canada, Dalhousie University.

Photo by Karolyn Smardz Frost

**Afua Cooper** is a multidisciplinary scholar, author, and artist. Her thirteen books range across such genres as history, poetry, fiction, and children's literature. Her indomitable research on slavery and Black history has made her one of the leading figures in African Canadian studies, and the authority on Canadian slavery. Her book *The Hanging of Angelique: The Untold Story of Slavery in Canada and the Burning of Old Montreal,* broke new ground in the study of Canadian and Atlantic slavery. Dr. Cooper led the "Universities Studying Slavery" initiative at Dalhousie University, and was the lead author of the subsequent report, *Lord Dalhousie's History on Slavery and Race.* These initiatives revealed the connections between the Canadian academy and the Atlantic slaving systems. In 2021, Dr. Cooper was appointed as the Canadian representative on the International Scientific Committee that advises UNESCO on implementation of its Slave Route Project, a main objective of which is to conduct research on the Transatlantic slavery system and its legacies. A celebrated poet, Dr. Cooper was awarded the Portia White Prize in 2020, Nova Scotia's highest recognition for the arts. She is also the winner of the J.M. Abraham Atlantic Poetry Award for her poetry book *Black Matters.* Afua Cooper currently teaches in the Faculty of Arts and Social Sciences at Dalhousie University, where she holds a Killam Research Chair, and is leading the project A Black People's History of Canada.

Photo by Norm Frost

**Dr. Karolyn Smardz Frost** is an archaeologist, historian, and award-winning author. In 1985, she and her team at the Toronto Board of Education's Archaeological Resource Centre uncovered the first Underground Railroad site in Canada. Karolyn is the author, co-author, or co-editor of five acclaimed volumes on African Canadian history. Her biography of freedom seekers Lucie and Thornton Blackburn, *I've Got a Home in Glory Land: A Lost Tale of the Underground Railroad* (2007) won the Governor General's Literary Award for Non-Fiction. She holds the 2018 Mathieu Da Costa Award from the Ontario Black History Society for contributions to African Canadian history education. In 2012–13, Karolyn served as Canadian Bicentennial Visiting Professor at Yale University. Now living in Wolfville, Nova Scotia, Karolyn is an adjunct professor at Acadia and Dalhousie Universities, an Affiliated Research Scholar at the University of Buffalo Archaeology Lab, and the Senior Research Fellow for A Black People's History of Canada project at Dalhousie University.